WHAT'S YOUR BQ™?

WHAT'S YOUR BQ™?

Learn How 35 Companies Add Customers, Subtract Competitors, and Multiply Profits with

Brand Quotient™

Written by
Sandra Sellani

W Business Books

an imprint of New Win Publishing
a division of Academic Learning Company, LLC

Library of Congress Cataloging-in-Publication Data

Sellani, Sandra.
  What's your BQ? : learn how 35 companies add customers, subtract competitors, and
multiply profits with Brand Quotient / Sandra Sellani.
     p. cm.
  ISBN 0-8329-5002-5 (hardcover)
  1. Brand name products. 2. Brand name products--Management. I. Title.
HD69.B7S367 2007
658.8'27--dc22

                                    2006034772

Dedications

This is dedicated to those whose
inspiration & encouragement made this book possible:

Mentors
John Klymshyn, who never stops pushing me,
David Frosh for his constant mentorship and encouragement,
Steve Gardner & Jim Jacobus for their kindness, honesty and guidance,
Scott Sherman whose strategy class of 2003 inspires me to this day
Dr. Jay Barney – whose work has changed my business and my
life forever,

Family
My parents, John and Angie Sellani, for their love and support,
My better half, my twin sister, Susan Hosage,
who is far away but always in my heart,
My nephew John Sellani, who put up with my complete unavailability
during the writing of this book

Colleagues
Joe Stammen, David Ebeling, Megain Monfort and Kymberlee Black

Friends
Michael Neufeld, who after 15 years, can still make me laugh until I cry,
Bobbie Theodore, Rochelle Cowper and Kymberlee Black, Lois Fox,
and C.M., my lifelong friends,
& Tom Popp, my love.

Contents

SECTION III: Planning Your Brand Strategy

Foreword

One Important Question

Early in my career I received some great advice from a very successful CEO who said, "The most compelling question a business needs to ask itself is – What is our unfair competitive advantage?" The reality is that without an unfair competitive advantage the company is destined to compete primarily on price and possibly fall into a place known as "commodity hell."

I have spent more than twenty years creating or evolving brands for clients and the question of unfair competitive advantage still stumps even the best and most prepared corporate executives. The problem is that often, when the company was formed, it had an unfair advantage; however, as the company grew or grew older, it became difficult to maintain. This is why brand, which defines the distinction of "unfair competitive advantage," must evolve over time. There are too many factors to become complacent in this regard – the competition catches up, the marketplace changes, there is a revolving door of change at the executive level or there is just not a corporate culture of continuing innovation. It is imperative for companies to constantly challenge themselves to keep this competitive edge and very importantly - aggressively claim their differentiation through a consistent branding program in the marketplace.

Much has been said about the global economy, but its existence necessitates creating a sustainable competitive advantage and a clear promise of distinction. That is also why brand distinction should be a corporate initiative and not just a marketing initiative. The CEO and executive team must own the brand for it to be successful. And there are many reasons why.

A branding strategy will never reach its potential unless it is completely aligned with the business strategy and the internal alignment of the entire organization. Secondly, the company's financial valuation is greatly affected by the intangibles (brand) within the organization. In many cases the brand value of the company is greater than the book value of the company. On average the intangible value of stocks traded on the New York Stock Exchange represent more than 60 percent of the market value. For this reason alone, it is clear why the CEO should be placing a huge emphasis on the ability to direct the corporate brand. For private companies, the ability to own a clear and defendable position in the marketplace can not only drive top line sales and bottom line profit but also position the company to be very attractive for an acquisition – at a premium price.

I know that some of you already understand the importance of building the brand, but what you may not know is the process of doing so. This is where *What's Your BQ*^{TM}*?* is so different than most branding books on the market. Sandra provides key insights and practical examples into the process of building a corporate brand that can truly create an unfair competitive advantage.

In *What's Your BQ*^{TM}*?* you have been given the opportunity to measure the strength of your company's brand and test how your brand stacks up against other companies in your category. Sandra also provides great examples of companies who have developed a unique brand strategy that has propelled them to success. No matter what category your business is in, you will find that many of these strategies will have relevance and could spark insights for the creation of a new brand or the evolution of a current brand.

I welcome you to apply the practical insights outlined in this book to create unlimited success for your business.

RiechesBaird, a business/brand consulting firm that builds the market value of B2B brands through business strategy, brand development and integrated marketing, is ranked among "The Top 10 B2B Agencies in the U.S."

—Ryan Rieches,

CEO RiechesBaird

Preface

"The future ain't what it used to be."
—Yogi Berra

Remember not too long ago when branding seemed to be a simple concept? In the minds of many businesses, it was just a logo, a color or a catchy tagline. But increased competition for the attention of the consumer has made branding a much more sophisticated venture. I meet a lot of business owners who are confused and overwhelmed with the prospect of branding their companies. And for good reason.

Branding is far too important a job to be left to the marketing department. It's everyone's responsibility, but most of all, the brand champion of the company must be the company's leader – whether you call yourself CEO, president or founder, you will set the tone for the brand because only you touch every area of the corporation. If you are a brand champion, you will ensure that it is incorporated into every department, every initiative.

Many companies do not consider brand strategy when creating corporate strategy but they are one and the same. Branding and strategy are as inextricably interwoven as a complex tapestry and separating them would snag, flaw and deteriorate the company's overall image and function. As the company's leader, you should ensure that decisions are made on the basis of whether or not they support or negate the brand. Likewise, brand decisions should be made on whether or not it supports the strategic vision.

The method I will use to help you build a brand is the same method used to help business leaders create strategies for a sustainable competitive advantage. The system, called the VRIO model, was created by Dr. Jay Barney of Ohio State University, who created it to transform the wisdom of academia into a business world which demands practicality and execution. His method is the "e=mc^2" of businesses –simple yet brilliant. When I learned about it, I wanted to share it with the entire business community, and in fact, I teach Dr. Barney's model regularly to business owners throughout the country to give them a systematic means to build their business. If you are like these business leaders, you will find this model to be refreshing in its simplicity but powerful in its execution.

I am thankful that Dr. Barney has given his blessing to allow me to share my interpretation of this powerful strategy tool for branding. But it's not something that can be left in a text book – it begs to be used and once you learn about it, you'll be hooked. By bringing brand in alignment with strategy, every department within your company will fly in unequivocal formation. You will give your company an ability to have a sustainable competitive advantage in a competitive marketplace.

People Who Will Benefit from Reading this Book

- CEOs, presidents, owners of small to medium sized businesses (you will also want to share this with your management team members and VPs as branding is their responsibility as well)

- Private practice professionals who must sell their services – like lawyers, accountants, CPAs, physicians

- Salespeople who are independent contractors, and therefore, running their own small businesses

Acknowledgements

I would like to thank and acknowledge the business owners and
representatives who have enabled me to share their stories.
You are the people that make the business world an exciting place.
You are the risk takers, the visionaries, the dreamers.
You are my heroes.

Introduction

"Good instincts tell you what to do long before
your head has figured it out."
—Michael Burke

I am fascinated by small business owners with successful brands. When you consider the fact that 80 percent of all brands die upon introduction and 10 percent die within the following five years, it's hard not to look at these people in awe. Who are they? How did they get that great idea? How did they bring it to fruition? Do they have some special knowledge, skill or training? Were they simply in the right place at the right time? What is that seemingly elusive "it" factor that has brought them from obscurity to success?

Chances are, they did start with a great idea, but it takes more than a great idea to be successful. And it takes more than a great idea to have sustainable success. The thirty-five companies in this book have many common traits. They are risk takers. They did research before starting their companies, but didn't over analyze—they acted. They had the ability to quickly change their strategy if it wasn't working and build on it if it was. They persisted. They never lost site of their goal.

But perhaps you've done all those things in your business and still feel that something is missing, something that will give you that extra edge over your competition. The "it" factor you're looking for just might be something else I observed in these companies; they had a remarkable gut instinct about building their brands. They had remarkable Brand Quotients.

What's a Brand Quotient? In its purest sense, it's that innate ability to get into the minds and often the hearts of your prospects—and stay there. It's the ability to set your company or product apart from the competition even when you're surrounded by competitors who have bigger budgets, a larger sales team, or who claim they do the same thing as you do. It's the ability to create memorable experiences for your clients over and over again, experiences so compelling that they will keep coming back for more, tell others about your company and even pay more for your products or services than they would for your competitors.

The leaders of these thirty-five companies seem to have instincts that made all of this happen and more. It's a quality I just wanted to bottle and sell to the world. But the closest I could come was to develop a Brand Quotient Test. The test includes the things these business leaders did instinctively. It also introduces concepts from the VRIO model, that most of these companies may not be consciously using, but seem to instinctively make a part of their businesses. And finally, it includes successful practices that I have used and observed in more than twenty years as a marketing executive.

By taking the test, you can get an immediate snapshot of your own Brand Quotient. You can immediately identify your strengths and weaknesses and know where to make changes. But what if you don't have those same gut instincts of the thirty-five business leaders outlined in this book? What if you don't like your score? Can Brand Quotient be learned?

It can. Unlike Intelligence Quotient (IQ), which we have little ability to change, Brand Quotient (BQ) can be raised and, in doing so, you can have a powerful impact on the success and longevity of your company.

After reading this book, you will have the ability to create a remarkable brand for your company. It's not about spending a lot of money. It's not about huge advertising campaigns. It's not about being the biggest company in your market. It's about a step by step process to build a brand and a strategy that anyone can learn and master with any size company.

After you take the test, I will teach you a simple process for building a brand that is truly unique from your competitors. I will help you to experience the importance of having a point of differentiation for your company. I will also guide you through the process of developing your company's differentiation strategy and tactics through a technique I call "brandstorming." As a result, you will be able to create a customized brand plan that you can implement immediately.

Your participation in the exercises in this book can have a profound impact on your company if you put it into practice, and the practicality of the system will enable you to do just that.

In addition to their great instincts about branding, I have selected the thirty-five companies in this book because their stories are so inspirational and because they did remarkable things without being the biggest in their respective categories.

Get ready to be inspired, not only by what they've done, but by what you can and will do. Once you read this book, you will look at your company with new eyes and have a renewed energy in bringing this system into being for extraordinary results. I am honored to join you on this journey.

SECTION I:
Identifying Your Brand

CHAPTER 1
It's About Them

"But enough about me, let's talk about you.
What do YOU think of me?"
—Bette Midler as CC Bloom in *Beaches*

If you were fortunate enough to see Bette Midler's delightful performance in the movie *Beaches*, you undoubtedly remember the laughter that followed her endearing, but completely self-absorbed statement. Yet, every day, as business owners, salespeople or marketers, we often fall into the same "let's talk about me" approach.

We can't wait to tell everyone about our company, our services, and our products. Our websites begin with an "about us" section. We give sales pitches that highlight our features and benefits. We place advertisements that talk about who we are and what we do. We give clients our track record, bios, testimonials and more. Yet, the last thing people want to hear about is us; first they want to hear about themselves and their needs. Then, they will be open to hearing about how our business can meet their needs. Our prospects need to know that we already know who they are. We understand them. We've done our homework and we know their needs better than they do. They must be affected by us and our words. They must feel a response to our messages. Sometimes that response is laughter. Sometimes it's intrigue. It can be fear or sadness or curiosity. If we can make them experience something that is visual, emotional, rational or cultural, we've started to make an impression in their mind. If we can keep that impression there for any length of time, we are beginning to create a brand. If we keep positive impressions and loyalty in their mind for a significant amount of time, we have created a brand.

What's the Difference?

Five years ago, when I began working with Sperry Van Ness Commercial Real Estate Advisors, a Southern California based brokerage firm, we were conducting business primarily in the Southwestern states and did about $2.1 billion in property sales with 100 brokers. Today, the company has grown to a national brand with $9.5 billion in property sales, more than 800 brokers, and is still growing. How could this happen in five short years? No one knew who we were in other parts of the country; in fact, no one cared. The company had been in existence since 1987. What happened in those five years that was so different?

What changed was that we started to communicate our strongest point of differentiation. It had been there all along, but we organized the corporation to leverage it to its fullest. The president of the company, David Frosh, co-founder Randy Sperry and I traveled to five cities each month speaking to people face to face about this compelling point of differentiation and people responded. They couldn't help but respond. We had a powerful story to tell that was in their best interests. We used that point of differentiation in everything we did from our sales pitches to our marketing materials to the decisions we made as a company. The growth was unprecedented in the history of the company which had already been in business for fifteen years prior to the national expansion. Our competitors had been in business far longer, had budgets that dwarfed ours, and had significantly better name recognition. But we had a compelling competitive difference.

It is differentiation that will give you a voice that can be heard in a sea of competitive cacophony. It is differentiation that will keep your company in the minds, hearts, and souls of your clients. It is differentiation that will give you a sustainable competitive advantage in a marketplace flooded by "we can do that too" competitors. And that differentiation is achieved through branding. And the better you are at building that brand, the greater the impact of its differentiation. When you think of your differentiation, think of it as your clients will perceive it. It's not enough to be a differentiator to you. Remember, it's all about them.

CHAPTER 2
Do You Know Where
You Stand?

Chances are, your clients like you. They're doing business with you. But can you say with conviction that they will stay with you over the long term? What about your prospects? Will they like you once they've heard what you have to say? After all, we learned that in marketing and branding, it's all about them, the clients and prospects. Those who are happy with you today can be lured away by another brand that offers just a bit more or positions themselves a bit differently. And prospects may not even want to give you a chance unless you can give them a compelling reason to do so. How does your company rate in the ability to get prospects and retain clients over the long term? Sometimes, it's hard to be objective. It's good to get a second opinion, in this case, the BQ test.

For those of you who have test anxiety, have no fear. Remember you can and will improve your BQ Score! The purpose of the BQ test is to help you determine your natural Brand Quotient: where you and your company stand before you begin to use the systems outlined in the book. There are three things you should know about the test:

1. **A low score does not mean your company is doomed.** There are a lot of thriving companies that still need to work on certain areas of their branding. The goal of getting a higher score on the test is that

the higher the score, the greater the strength of the brand and the greater the likelihood that your company will have a sustainable competitive advantage in your market.

2.   One size does not fit all. Since there are different types of people who will be taking this test—small and mid sized businesses, a one-man operation, an independent sales professional, or someone with a professional practice, like a physician, trying to brand their company—there will be certain questions that vary to meet each group's individual needs. These questions will have special notes after them, instructing you how to respond in your particular circumstance.

3.   BQ can and will be improved! So much of branding is impacted by our awareness of branding issues. I encourage you to take this test now as a baseline and again three months and six months after you implement the strategies outlined in the book to see how you have improved. And you **WILL** improve if you incorporate these strategies. I've included multiple blank grids so you can do just that.

You can also take the **BQ** test online at *www.mybrandquotient.com.* The advantage to taking it online is that the **BQ** grid will be automatically generated for you. You'll also be able to see how your **BQ** ranks with other companies in your category.

The test in the book will involve manually plotting your scores on the **BQ** grid, and it's always fun when you get to write in your book. And *do* write—don't be like my friend who doesn't like to even bend the spine of a book when he reads (he also has the cleanest house I've ever seen, but that's the subject of another book). Scribble, doodle, highlight, dog ear and make it your own. It's a part of you. It is your guide. Experience it. Live it. Use it as a coaster. Besides, if it gets messy, you can buy more.

The BQ Test

Instructions:

The BQ Test includes Four Categories with 10 questions each:

I. Brand Strategy

II. Brand Alignment

III. Brand Communication

IV. Brand Execution

Assign a score from "1 to 5" for each statement based on how true the statement is (i.e., if the statement is true 100 percent of the time, the score would be "5", 20 percent of the time, the score would be "1"). At the end of each category you will have the opportunity to assess your Brand Quotient for each category and as a whole.

BQ Category I: Brand Strategy

____ My company's product or service has a strong point of difference from my competitor's product/service.

____ I can summarize my brand in one word and so can my clients (i.e. Volvo = safety). If so, give yourself a "5". If you and your clients can summarize your brand in one statement, (i.e. "The Ultimate Driving Machine") give yourself a "4".

____ The value of my product or service does not show a current threat of being outdated by new products or technologies.

____ I regularly review my points of differentiation to ensure that they are not being imitated by my competitors.

____ I have a clear understanding of competitors' strengths and weaknesses.

____ I have a plan to help my brand survive if it is imitated by competitors.

____ I have proprietary methods, technologies or other elements which other companies do not.

____ My point of differentiation is difficult for my competitors to imitate.

____ My point of differentiation is costly for my competitors to imitate, either in terms of time, money, culture or logistics.

____ I am building every level of the organization—operations, finance, marketing, administration, pricing—around the brand.

Total Score for Category I: Brand Strategy (add all numbers) _____
BQ Score for Category I: (Brand Strategy Score x2) _____

BQ Category II: Brand Alignment

____ My brand is linked to my business's vision statement, culture, values, and overall strategy.

____ Employee reviews include reinforcement and rewards for supporting, communicating and championing the brand. *(Note: If you are a salesperson or a one-man operation, give yourself a "5" for this)*

____ My employees can articulate or demonstrate how our offering differs from the competition. *(Note: If you are a salesperson or a one-man operation, rank this on how it applies to you)*

____ My sales staff communicates our differentiators to the client in a consistent manner to show competitive advantages. *(Note: If you are a salesperson or a one-man operation, rank this on how it applies to you)*

____ Customers buy from me not just for the product but for a unique experience they get when using the product.

____ I regularly survey my customers to ensure that I am providing a product or service that is valuable and relevant.

____ I incorporate feedback from prospects, customers, vendors and the media to improve my offering.

____ My management team buys into the brand offering and actively incorporates it into their daily operations. *(Note: If you are a salesperson or a one-man organization, rank this on how it applies to you)*

____ My management team makes decisions based on whether or not it will support or negate the brand. *(Note: If you are a salesperson or a one-man operation, rank this on how it applies to you)*

____ I am not the low price leader in my category.

Total Score for Category II: Brand Alignment (add all numbers) _____
BQ Score for Category II: (Brand Alignment Score x2) _____

BQ Category III: Brand Communications

____ My marketing materials clearly communicate my company's brand and points of competitive differentiation.

____ My company is free of scandal and negative publicity.

____ All marketing materials—print, electronic, web—have continuity in their colors, images, and messaging.

____ I leverage my brand with publicity and regular contacts with the media.

____ I have and enforce a graphic branding standards manual that explains how each element of my brand should be dealt with in the operation of the business (i.e., colors of logo, layout of graphics on stationery, font sizes to be used) to ensure that all graphic elements of my brand are consistent.

____ The quality of my marketing materials is equal to or greater than the quality of my services.

____ My sales team does not create or customize their materials in a way that alters the brand image or message. *(Note: If you are a salesperson or a one-man operation, rate this on how it applies to you)*

____ My management team reinforces brand messages in their staff meetings and interactions. *(Note: If you are a salesperson or a one-man operation, rate this on how it applies to you)*

____ My messages, ads, graphics, and colors have remained consistent over time, unless there was a specific change strategy in place.

____ My sales team uses an emotional component to encourage and reinforce use of the brand. *(Note: If you are a salesperson or a one-man operation, rate this on whether or not you employ this tactic)*

Total Score for Category III: Brand Comm. (add all numbers) _____

BQ Score for Category III: (Brand Communications Score x2) _____

BQ Category IV: Brand Execution

___ My company's phone is answered by a pleasant, knowledgeable individual who can quickly and amiably meet the caller's needs.

___ I understand that my brand exists only in the minds of my customers and prospects.

___ My company resolves customer service issues promptly and efficiently to the client's satisfaction.

___ I regularly receive superior customer satisfaction ratings when I survey my customers and prospects.

___ I keep my offerings relevant by keeping up with technology, market shifts and customer needs.

___ My company's products are delivered consistently regardless of whether they are accessed on the web or in person.

___ My client's interaction with my product, services, and employees is positive, unique, and memorable.

___ My product or service is easy to use, find or access.

___ My clients regularly refer others to my company.

___ My clients use my services consistently and do not flip back and forth between me and my competitors.

Total Score for Category IV: Brand Execution (add all numbers) _____

BQ Score for Category IV: (Brand Execution Score x2) _____

BQ Score Grid:

Enter your BQ Score in Each Category

Category I: Brand Strategy _____%

Category II: Brand Alignment _____%

Category III: Brand Communications _____%

Category IV: Brand Execution _____%

YOUR BRAND QUOTIENT Overall Average (Add BQ
Percentage Scores from categories I – IV, then divide by 4) _____%

Scoring:

95 – 100%	A	Outstanding
90 – 94%	A-	Excellent
85 – 89%	B	Very Good
80 - 84%	B-	Good
75 – 79%	C	Average
70 – 74%	C-	Below Average
65 – 69%	D	Poor
60 – 64%	D-	At Risk
Below 60	F	Fail

Plotting Your Score on the BQ Grid

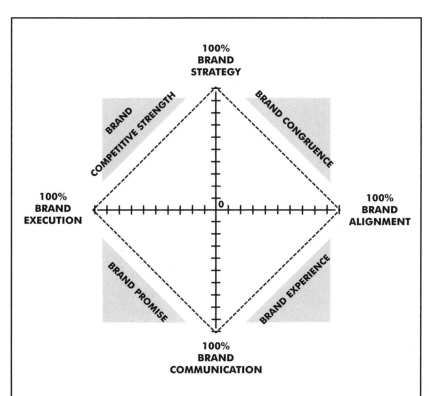

For each of the four scores, place a dot in the appropriate location on the BQ Grid. For example, if your scores were as follows:

>Brand Strategy: 80%
>Brand Execution 65%
>Brand Communication: 85%
>Brand Alignment 90%
>**Your BQ is 80%**

Your grid would look like this:

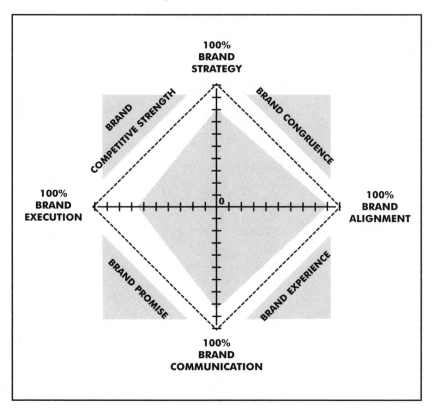

Plot your BQ Score Here

Place a dot on the line that corresponds to your score. Your Brand Strategy Score dot will be placed on the grid mark in the center. If you received a 50 percent, then count up from the center to the 5th gridline. Do the same with Brand Execution, Brand Communications, and Brand Alignment. When you have put your dots on the grid, draw a line to connect the dots and shade the area inside the borders of your drawing. The darker areas within the dotted lines show strengths; the white areas show where improvement is needed. The closer your shading is to the dotted line, the stronger the function. A perfect score, of course would be if the dotted lines were filled in completely.

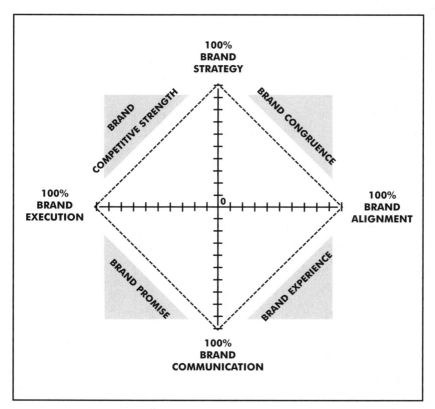

Interpreting Your Score

Your BQ score in each category and overall will give you a general assessment of how your company ranks in that category. In the example above, your score is

Brand Strategy: 80% (B-, Good)
Brand Execution: 65% (D, Poor)
Brand Communication: 85% (B, Very Good)
Brand Alignment: 90% (A-, Excellent)
Your BQ is 80% (B-, Good)

The grid will give you a visual of your areas of strength and weakness. The dotted line would represent a perfect score. The more color that fills in your grid, the higher the areas of strength.

What does it mean?

Brand Strategy: The plan for incorporating the brand to support the strategic goals of the company and make a strong impact in the mind of the consumer.

Brand Execution: Refers to your ability to carry out the elements of your brand strategy.

Brand Communication: Refers to your ability to communicate internally and externally your brand's points of differentiation to your clients, prospects, employees and other stakeholders in a consistent manner.

Brand Alignment: Refers to your ability to create a brand with internal and external alignment. In other words, the promise you make to the consumer must be kept by the internal people of your organization.

We will go into each of these in more detail later in the book. For now, at a glance, you can get an overall idea of how you do in each of these areas, but each of these areas impact each other as well. Each of the quadrants shows which elements of your company's brand will be impacted by your scores. The following are some examples:

Brand Strategy & Execution will impact your Competitive Strength Quadrant– This quadrant shows your ability to sustain your brand over the long term. If you have a high score in strategy and a low score in execution, you will have poor competitive strength because even though you've planned how to position your company, you are not carrying it through to your clients and prospects, you have a competitive weakness. If you score low in strategy and high in execution, you will be implementing a strategy that is undefined. You may have a temporary advantage, but without defining a clear strategy, you will be unable to get a true assessment of your competitive position and future execution of the brand may be faulty.

Brand Execution and Communication will impact your Brand Promise – The brand promise is the promise you make to your clients and prospects about what you will deliver to them. If you promise a remarkable experience, but don't deliver, you will have broken your promise. Your clients will feel cheated or betrayed. If you have an excellent brand experience, but don't tell your clients about it, brand promise will be unspoken. You may generate word of mouth (WOM) business and this can be sustained over time, but by building a communication plan, you may be able to gain a stronger competitive edge.

Brand Communication and Brand Alignment will impact your client's Brand Experience – If you communicate that you have a particular type of experience to employees, but send another message to clients, you are giving them an inconsistent and confusing experience with your company.

Brand Alignment and Strategy will impact Brand Congruence – If your internal and external brand messages are consistent, your clients and prospect's experiences with your brand will be too.

Brand Congruence Matrices

	High Strategy	Low Strategy
High Execution	High Competitive Strength	Poor or Temporary Competitive Strength
Low Execution	Poor Competitive Strength	No Competitive Strength

	High Execution	Low Execution
High Communication	Brand Promise Kept - will likely generate new and repeat business.	Brand Promise Broken – likely to lose customers and create negative word of mouth communication.
Low Communication	Brand Promise Experienced but Not Communicated – may delay company success.	Brand Promise Never Communicated. - not likely to generate new or repeat business.

	High Communication	Low Communication
High Alignment	Powerful Brand Experience – brand will be reinforced.	Brand promise will be kept but not reinforced in outgoing ads, press releases or other contacts with your consumers.
Low Alignment	Poor Brand Experience	No Brand Experience

	High Alignment	Low Alignment
High Strategy	High Brand Congruence	Brand Promise Broken.
Low Strategy	Employee Confusion as to how to carry out the brand promise.	No Brand Congruence.

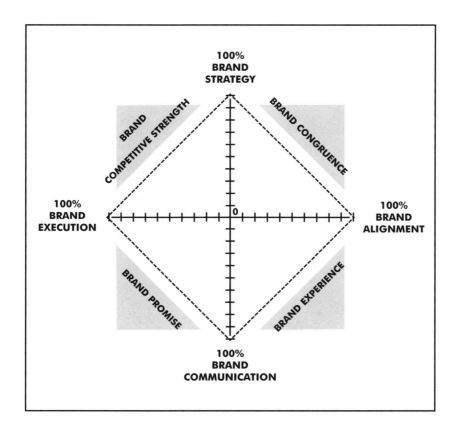

CHAPTER 3
The Brand Illusion

*"The very first law in **advertising** is to avoid the concrete promise and cultivate the delightfully vague."*

—Bill Cosby

If you've ever purchased Morton Salt, Clorox Bleach or Evian Water, you've experienced it. It's the brand illusion – the phenomenon that occurs when you believe that one brand has a powerful difference over another brand - when there is really no difference at all. This difference tells you that the name brand is superior. It tells you to pay more for the superior product. But in the case of Morton, Clorox and Evian, you're paying more money for the brand – because these products are no different than their generic counterparts. They are commodities. A commodity is a product that is so like other products in its category that the two are interchangeable. Salt, bleach and water are commodities – until someone makes us think otherwise.

Salt is sodium chloride (NaCl). Morton Salt has exactly the same components as any other table salt - yet you paid about 77 percent more for the Morton brand over the generic brand. But don't feel bad, you're in good company. The Morton brand has dominated the salt market since 1848. Morton Salt actually did start with a point of differentiation. They were the first company to create a salt that wouldn't get clumps even in damp weather, allowing it to pour freely. They created a differentiator through their slogan "When it rains, it pours" and personified it with the Morton Umbrella Girl who displays the free flowing salt while walking in the rain. Clearly, other companies have long since been able to copy that differentiator and make free flowing salt, making salt a commodity once again. But consumers developed an association with the brand and now pay more.

And what about the bleach – or sodium hypochlorite (NaClO)? It's composed of the same elements as that generic brand bleach, but you paid about 42 percent less for it than Clorox, which continues to be a brand leader worldwide.

And let's not forget about water, or H20. You paid as much as 169 percent more for that bottle of Evian than for a store name or generic brand. In fact, Americans spent $10 billion in 2005 on a commodity that we can all get for free. And what most people don't realize is that the regulation of bottled water is less restrictive than the regulation of tap water. At least one-fourth of all bottled-water brands obtain their water from the municipal water systems, including Coca-Cola Corporation's Dasani brand, and PepsiCo's, Aquafina brand. Additionally, studies have consistently revealed a surprising finding in blind taste tests with tap and bottled waters. "Across the board, people can't tell the difference," said Bryan Hirsch, a spokesman for Corporate Accountability. "Over 1,000 people have taken the test in more than a dozen cities, and the overwhelming sentiment from them is that they've been duped."

Branded commodities appear different, better or more desirable than their non-branded counterparts. The bottom line is branding yields a perceived difference, even if there is no difference. Lack of branding yields no perceived difference even if there is a difference.

You've also experienced the brand illusion when you purchase other products in which there is a difference, but the difference you're paying for may not be the difference you're getting. Let's drink on it. How about an imported beer? You might think that beers really *are* different, they're *not* commodities. So if you were willing to pay $1.50 for a 24 ounce bottle of Budweiser, it would only make sense that you would pay more for an imported beer like Sapporo, marketed as "Japan's Oldest Premium Beer." A 22 ounce bottle is $2.99, double the price of the Budweiser for 2 ounces less product. But it's worth it to pay twice as much for a beer imported all the way from Japan. The only problem is Sapporo beer distributed in the United

States is brewed by Molson - in Canada.

Knowing what we know about the brand illusion, we are still compelled to buy brand names and pay more for them not because of what they say about the product, but for what they say about us. Sometimes it's a little bit more, as in the case of salt. Sometimes it's a lot more, like a luxury vehicle. We can't help but pay more, because we as consumers don't buy products, we buy brands.

We buy brands because we identify with them and we buy brands because of what we *think* they say about us. Does driving a five-figure Jaguar tell others, we're special, wealthy or even "gorgeous" as their current ad campaign indicates? Does drinking a $3.00 cup of Starbucks coffee mean we are upwardly mobile, busy business professionals? Does wearing a pair of $900 Manolo Blahnik shoes mean we're as stylish as Sarah Jessica Parker's character, Carrie Bradshaw who made the brand a household name on HBO's *Sex and the City*? In some cases brands truly are different from their competitors; in other cases, they're not. But it doesn't really matter, because we will pay more for the differences in a brand whether or not the differentiation is real or *perceived*. That's the brand illusion.

So how does this apply to your business? The bottom line is you need a point of differentiation - real or perceived - to be a brand. People buy for two reasons: low price or differentiation. If you do not have a point of differentiation, prepare to be the low price leader. Now, you can have a low-price strategy. It's a legitimate strategy. But if low price is the only thing you have to offer, you had better be prepared to have the high volume necessary to generate a profit. Companies like Wal-Mart have done this successfully, but many small and medium sized businesses cannot achieve the amount of volume that can justify this strategy. Smaller retail stores often cannot compete on price with high volume retailers – so they must rely on differentiation. Many women shop at boutique clothing stores instead of larger retailers because of the quaint atmosphere, personal attention and unique items that can't be found in the high volume larger chains – and they pay more to do so. Boutiques have found a niche that will allow them to survive in the retail industry, not by competing on price with retail giants, but by using differentiation to capture a specific segment and psychographic within retail buyers.

If you want people to choose you for reasons other than "low cost," you need a differentiator. So when we go through the exercise of building your brand, we will build in a point of differentiation. Also know that in promoting your brand it is important to focus on only *one* point of differentiation. You want one word or concept associated with your brand. Anything else might be confusing. If Volvo, a brand associated with safety, suddenly started focusing on design, the public would be confused. It doesn't mean that they can't start creating uniquely styled cars, or develop new designs; it's just not what they should promote. If BMW started promoting themselves as "The Ultimate Safety Machine," people would be confused. By sticking with "The Ultimate Driving Machine," they can keep their branding intact. They can and do have safety features, but that's not how they lead. This is important because many companies want to talk about a long list of features and benefits right from the start. Learn that what you promote and what you offer can be different. Just stay consistent in what you promote to get people to remember and use your brand. Once they begin to use your brand, feel free to tell them about your other wonderful features and benefits, but don't bombard them in your advertising with your many traits.

Branding – the most overused and underrated term in business

Through the years, there have been business words that have been used to death until we don't want to use them anymore. Networking. Value added. Best practices. TQM. And now, branding. Everyone talks about branding and everyone seems to have a different definition. Marty Neumeier, Author of *The Brand Gap*, describes brand as a "gut feeling" that people have about your product, service or company. Al and Laura Ries define brand as "the ability to create in the mind of the prospect the perception that there is no other product on the market quite like yours." Duane Knapp, author of *The Brand Mindset* defines brand as "the internalized sum of all impressions, received by customers and consumers resulting in a distinctive position in their mind's eye based on perceived emotional and functional benefits." Which definition is correct? All of them. And there are more definitions.

My favorite definition is from Charles Pettis, President of Brand Solutions, Inc.: "Brand is a proprietary visual, emotional, rational, and cultural image that you associate with a product or service." It's a mouthful but it clarifies what branding is in the mind of the consumer. It's an all-encompassing definition because brand is an all-encompassing concept.

It doesn't matter if you are a mom and pop business, a salesperson or the president of a small or medium sized company. Your company has elements that fit into all of these categories – proprietary, visual, emotional, rational and cultural. Complete the elements grid on page 34.

Exercise 1 – What Are My Brand Elements?

List the elements that your company has in each category.

Instructions:

Proprietary: In the proprietary section, write anything your company has that is trademarked, copyrighted, intellectual property, or any other proprietary element of your business. This includes trademarked taglines, logos, technology, secret recipes, manufacturing or product design. As you will learn in a later exercise, these elements can be strong brand differentiators. You can cut and paste visuals into this section of the grid, such as a logo or specific colors, or you can just write them in.

Visual: Write, draw or cut and paste any element of your business that can be associated with your brand. It can be a logo, company colors, font styles or pictures of products. If you have multiple products, you may want to reference this (i.e., four hardware and six software products for point of service retailers). Visual can also include packaging for your products, or any other image that comes to mind that visually communicates your brand.

Emotional: You may think only certain products have emotional value: a beautiful car, a large screen TV, or a bottle of expensive Champagne. But every product can have an emotional impact. In residential real estate, the purchase of the home is often an emotional purchase because it is associated with family, security and a sense of pride. People get emotional about selling their homes. They get emotional about buying homes. But what about commercial real estate, is there an emotional element? People who buy and sell commercial real estate are looking for one thing – return on investment. If they lose money on a deal, it's emotional. Therefore, their decisions have an emotional component. No one wants to feel foolish because they've made a bad investment. No one wants to feel that they've compromised their earnings because they sold too soon or for too little. People who sell their commercial real estate can pay significant five and six figure commissions to their listing agent-that comes directly out of the profit from the sale of their property-paying that sum of money can make the property owner emotional, because they're letting go of their hard earned cash. So look at your business. Look at the transaction from beginning to end. Where will emotions come into play? Anger. Fear. Frustration. Joy. It's important to know. Any one of the columns of the matrix may be a differentiator, but very often, it's the emotional component that is among the strongest. You will often see the emotional elements of a brand emphasized in advertising.

Rational: What rational reasons are there for buying your product? Do you have better pricing? Easier access? More features? Is your product more robust? Is your product cheaper to operate? Does it replace multiple other products? List those adjectives or concepts in this section.

Cultural: What cultural elements are associated with your offering? Is your product cool? Is it conservative? Is it controversial? Does it make a statement about the person using it, making them smarter, more fashionable, more sophisticated?

The matrix exercise will help you look at your brand in a more comprehensive way. Your clients experience many thoughts and ideas about your brand, consciously and subconsciously. When you review the matrix, you will realize that your brand encompasses every experience that a consumer can have with your company. This grid also serves a second function: it's a benchmark for how you view your brand in comparison to how your clients view your brand. If you asked your customers to complete this grid, would they give the same answers? If there's a difference between the two, there is a disconnection between how you see your brand and how the consumer sees it. And since brand exists only in the mind of the consumer, their definition is correct.

What Are My Brand Elements?

Proprietary

```



```

Visual

```



```

Emotional

```



```

Rational

```



```

Cultural

```



```

You'll have an opportunity in the last section of this book "Putting it All Together" to use this information in the formulation of your company's brand strategy.

Here's a sample grid for a fictitious company to serve as an example.

Proprietary

Piano Works Training Studios - "The key to your musical success."
The studio is the only one to develop Mozart+ an award winning training method which helps children learn three times as fast as traditional methods.

Visual

Studio is decorated completely in black and white.
Posters of classical musicians on the walls.
Times New Roman, 12 pt font is used in the logo and in all marketing materials.

Emotional

Parents want their children to learn to play but cost is sometimes a concern.
Joy and pride associated with playing well.
Fear that children may miss an opportunity if they don't start at an early age.

Rational

Learning an instrument has been linked to improved math scores. This is something children can continue into their adulthood. It's an opportunity for the child to use their leisure time effectively, instead of playing video games. Method facilitates faster learning. It may ensure early success in the program and greater likelihood of practicing and improving.

Cultural

Musical aptitude is an admirable quality. It is a sophisticated and difficult task which others will admire in me or my child.

The sample grid encompasses a variety of concepts that the prospect or client might associate with the product.   These items will come into play as we dig deeper into defining the brand.

CHAPTER 4
Who are You?

"Knowledge of the self is the mother of all knowledge."
—Kahlil Gibran

Exercise #1: Four Questions

The first exercise may seem too simple at first, but, in fact, the way you define your company and the business you are in can completely alter who your competition is, who your clients are and what your brand message is. And, you may learn that the way you define your company varies within your organization. The questions that you will answer in this section are:

What business are you in?

Who are your competitors?

Who are your clients?

What do you sell?

Seem simple enough? That's what the people of Service Corporation of America thought when those questions were asked of them by their consultant. They hired the prolific business expert, author and consultant Peter Drucker, who spent his career studying business management. Drucker, who had the ability to bring simplicity to complex business issues, gave them information they never expected. The story, as told to me by a former student of

Drucker demonstrates how answering a simple question may not be as simple as you think.

Drucker's first question to the board was simple enough: What business are you in? Service Corporation of America was a provider of janitorial services. When Drucker presented the question to each person around the boardroom table, he got a variety of answers from the team, none of them correct, according to Drucker. Was it a janitorial business? What it a service organization? Drucker told them that they didn't know what business they were in, and this was the source of their problems. He then asked them to consider if they might be in the business of taking otherwise unemployable people and turning them into productive members of society. That's a bold statement, but one that became the definition of the company's business that flourished as a result of his direction.

Can you see that how you answer the question of "what business are you in" can not only bring clarity to all members of the organization, but can also dramatically impact the answers to the other three questions on the grid? For example, Southwest Airlines does not describe itself as being in the airline industry. President Colleen Barrett describes Southwest as "a customer service organization that just happens to fly airplanes." Even their mission statement does not mention the word airline! It reads, "The mission of Southwest Airlines is dedication to the highest quality of Customer Service delivered with a sense of warmth, friendliness, individual pride, and company spirit."

Are you brave enough to ask key members of your company what business you are in? Perhaps it's an easy answer, perhaps not. Start by completing the grid on the next page – by yourself. Once you know your answers, I encourage you to share them in front of a group of key people in your company. The answers might surprise you.

What business are we in?	Who are our competitors?
Make sure your management team agrees on this – the answer is not always as obvious as you think.	*Based on knowing what business you are in you may define your competitors differently.*

Who are our clients?	What do we sell?
Based on what business you are in, you may want to consider if you are looking at all your clients. Also consider media vendors as part of your client list. They can be brand champions or sabotage the brand, based on how you work with them.	*Southwest sees their product as customer service, not air travel. This is an important distinction that must be understood before you can define your brand.*

Example Grid: The following grid illustrates the questions answered by our fictitious company:

What business are we in?	Who are our competitors?
We teach piano to children and adults, including lessons for new and advanced players.	*ABC Piano Training* *"I'll be Bach" Piano Studios* *"Going for Baroque" Piano Lessons for Adults*

Who are our clients?	What do we sell?
Children beginning at the age of 6 through adults.	*The ability to create a mastery of musical proficiency through a method that allows people to become successful more quickly than through traditional methods.*

Your Grid

What business are we in?	Who are our competitors?

Who are our clients?	What do we sell?

Exercise #2: The List

The matrix helped you to start thinking about the various elements of your company and we will refer to it throughout the course of the book. The next step is called "The List." The object of the list is to help you determine your company's true differentiators. It is only through differentiation that you can begin to have a sustainable competitive advantage. Many people who complete the list for the first time are surprised to find that what they thought were true brand differentiators were not different at all. They also find that they have been focusing their sales and marketing on these non-differentiators; something that will prevent you from gaining and sustaining a competitive advantage in your market.

The list consists of blanks. In each blank, write down what you believe to be your company's greatest points of differentiation. In other words, if I were to ask you why I should work with you instead of one of your competitors, what would you say? You can use your matrix to help you come up with ideas for the list. At this point, leave the boxes marked with "VRIO" empty. We will get to those in our next step.

I won't give you any more clues than this because I want these answers to be the most sincere answers you would give to a prospect. Please take the time to do this list because every exercise we do from this point forward will be based on this list.

The List

	The Things that differentiate me from my competitors are (list below)	V	R	I	O
1					
2					
3					
4					
5					
6					
7					
8					
9					
10					

Now that you've completed the list, we're going to put each item to the test. The test we're about to do will reveal which items of your list are true differentiators. The method we will use is from Dr. Jay Barney's VRIO model. This is the single most important thing I have learned in my entire vocational and educational experience. We're going to go into detail on the VRIO because I believe it is the crux of brand differentiation and competitive advantage.

Exercise #3: The VRIO Analysis

Dr. Jay Barney, Ohio State University Professor and author of *Gaining and Sustaining Competitive Advantage* created a model that has had a profound effect on my work in marketing.

As I sat in my graduate class at Pepperdine University, Professor Scott Sherman began to discuss the VRIO model. As I listened, I couldn't believe my ears. This strategic planning model applied in every way to branding. And it should – brand cannot be separated from strategy. Brand is strategy conveyed to your target audience. I started to realize that the applications of the VRIO model could be used in any situation where a company, a brand or even a salesperson needed a competitive edge. Today I'm applying the VRIO model to our list and to the branding process in general. It will give you a clarity that you have never had about your brand. And once you use it, you won't be able to think about your brand or strategy without it.

I had the pleasure of speaking with Dr. Barney and asked him about the model. He stated, "The model of VRIO predicts that the physical attributes of a product are almost never a source of sustained competitive advantage - but the brands – a relationship between a firm and its customers - can last for a very long time."

So let's see how your list holds up under the model. In order for each item to remain on your list, it must meet all four VRIO criteria.

V   Valuable

Each item on the list must be valuable. Now, that probably seems easy enough, but let me give you a new way of looking at the word value, because we all think our products and services are valuable. If you have a business and people are buying your products, there is probably some value to them – do you know what it is? What you think is valuable may be different from what your clients think is valuable. If you think people are coming to your restaurant because you have the best food in town, but they are actually coming because they like the social aspect, you might be using the wrong messaging in your advertising and promotions.

As you look through your list, think of value through your customer's eyes. If all items on your list are truly valuable, write "Yes" in the "V" box to the right and keep them on the list. Now it's time to move to "R".

R Rare

In addition to being valuable, each item on your list also has to be rare. What does this mean? It means something that your competitors do not have. For example, if you have a proprietary technology program that helps save your clients time and money, it is both valuable and rare and gets a "yes" in the "V" and the "R" boxes. This is where I start to see people crossing things off their list. Many people when creating their list will write things like "I provide quality products." If the word "Quality" is on your list, it should be crossed off. Quality is valuable, but it's not rare. People expect quality –it's important but it's not a differentiator. When I have salespeople make this list, they often write things like:

"I'll go the extra mile for you."

"I'm an expert in my market."

"I know my products."

Again, valuable qualities, but not rare. Unless your competitors had terrible service, have no clue about their market and no product knowledge, these items should be crossed off the list and a "no" should be put in the corresponding box. How are you doing so far? Still a few items left? It's time to move on to "I".

I Costly to Imitate

Your differentiators must be costly to imitate. Costly can mean in terms of time, money, infrastructure, or any other element that would make it difficult for your competitors to replicate what you are doing. Imitation can mean the death of a brand. Many products have been imitated and then failed to thrive because their imitators did a better job than they did of marketing and selling the product.

If your items are valuable, rare and costly to imitate, put a "yes" in these three boxes. If not, put a "no" in the appropriate boxes and cross the item off your list. Usually by this point, many people who do this list are down to nothing – don't worry. You can and should make the list again after reading the rest of the book. The exercise will change the way you view differentiators, as will our final "brandstorming" exercise. Let's move on to "O."

O Organizational Leverage

What does this mean? It means that every part of your organization communicates the brand. Are the items on your list being leveraged or exploited across the organization to maximize their potential in your organization? Dr. Barney offers an example of organizational leverage within Wal-Mart.

> ...much of Wal-Mart's continuing competitive advantage in the discount retailing industry can be attributed to its early entry into rural markets.

To exploit their geographic advantage, they had to implement systems that would organize the entire corporation around the advantage. One way was through an inventory control system. Barney adds,

> ...this inventory control system has enabled Wal-Mart to take full advantage of its rural locations by decreasing the probability of stock outs in those locations.

Another example is General Electric's Trivection technology. Their Trivection ovens cook food in a fraction of the time of traditional ovens. For example, a baked potato would take one hour and fifteen minutes to cook in a traditional oven and only seventeen minutes in the Trivection oven. A twenty-two pound turkey takes two hours with the GE Product and four hours with a traditional product. It's a powerful differentiator from a powerful brand.

But GE doesn't stop there. They leverage this feature by creating an oven that calculates the appropriate convection time once the user inputs the traditional cooking time. If the cook places the turkey in the oven and sets it for four hours (the traditional time to cook the turkey), the oven calculates the convection time (two hours) and displays the new, reduced time enabled by the Trivection technology. This is an example of organizing the customer experience around the brand. Not only does the product have cutting edge technology, it reminds the customer with each use exactly how the brand promise is being kept.

Does every part of your company operate by communicating the brand? Purchasing, distribution, product experience, phone greetings, accounts payable and receivable? Is everything working together to support that brand? If so, put a "yes" in the "O" box. If not, put a "no" and cross the item off of your list. Some companies have strengths that are their best kept secrets. Differentiators must be communicated consistently. I often see people who stop communicating their differentiators because they feel the need to change their message. They get bored with a tagline and want to change it. They get bored with the look of a direct mail piece and want to change it. Keep in mind that the way to cut through clutter is consistency and repetition.

How is your list? Are there any items left? If, so, great. You're well on your way to creating a brand. If not, don't worry. Our brandstorming exercise will give you more ideas.

Let's look at a sample list from our same fictitious company.

Piano Works VRIO List

	Differentiator	V	R	I	O
1	~~Quality piano training~~	Yes	No	No	No
2	~~Affordable pricing~~	Yes	No	No	No
3	~~Friendly Staff~~	Yes	No	No	No
4	~~Convenient location~~	Yes	No	No	No
5	~~Well-trained teachers~~	Yes	No	No	No
6	~~Beautiful studio~~	No	No	No	No
7	~~First lesson free~~	Yes	Yes	No	No
8	~~Convenient hours~~	Yes	Yes	No	No
9	~~Monthly student recitals~~	Yes	Yes	No	No
10	Proprietary Mozart+ Training Method	Yes	Yes	Yes	Yes

Piano Works has a lot of valuable qualities, but most are not rare. Of those that are rare, their competition could easily begin to imitate them – they can offer more convenient hours, give the first lesson free, and add monthly recitals for students. But the one item that met all four criteria of differentiation was the Mozart+ Training Method.

Valuable. It is valuable because it enables students to learn more quickly –early success can mean the student will stick with the program, become less frustrated, and make piano lessons a long term goal.

Rare. It is rare because Piano Works created this proprietary method and is the only studio that offers it.

Costly to Imitate. Other studios would have to create another method that could increase the learning speed of students. The Mozart+ program took ten years to research, test and develop. This could be costly for competitors to imitate in terms of the time and money it would take to create a program that would exceed the benefits of Mozart+.

Organizational Leverage. Piano Works does promote the Mozart+ program, but should look for new ways to keep this at the forefront. Their monthly recitals feature students who are proficient in difficult classical pieces that places them three to four years ahead of their traditionally trained counter-parts. The monthly recitals could showcase this factor. By making the events open to the public and giving the audience an understanding of the results of the system, they could better leverage the benefits of the program. But there are many other opportunities for Piano Works to exploit their strengths including media relations and franchising the method to other studios.

Implication of VRIO

How did you do at defining your brand differentiators? Do you have any items left on your list? If you don't, don't worry. I'll give you some good news – you only need one item to have a point of differentiation. In fact, you only *should* have one point of differentiation that you use to promote the brand.

Think about it. Volvo promotes one thing – safety. They may have other qualities that are admirable and even be valuable, rare and costly to imitate - but they promote safety. Even if you had ten items on your list that all met the VRIO criteria, you would not want to promote all ten. It's easier for con-sumers to focus on one point of differentiation. It doesn't mean that you can't offer them many things once they purchase your product, use your services, or arrive at your store, but your brand message should consistently focus on the point of differentiation as seen in their taglines.

The power of having a single point of differentiation in your brand message is that it will be more focused and memorable. For example, you could probably insert the tagline of each of the following companies by just being given the name – even if some of the companies are no longer emphasizing the tagline in their advertising, the message is already ingrained in your memory.

Other companies that brand with a single focus:

Company Name	Tagline or single point of focus
BMW	
Papa John's Pizza	
Hallmark	
GE	
DeBeers	
Nike	
Miller Lite	
L'Oreal	
Morton Salt	
Wheaties	
Wendy's	

See how many you got correct:

Company Name	Tagline or single point of focus
BMW	The Ultimate Driving Machine.
Papa John's Pizza	Better Ingredients. Better pizza.
Hallmark	When you care enough to send the very best.
GE	We bring good things to life.
DeBeers	A diamond is forever.
Nike	Just do it.
Miller Lite	Tastes great. Less filling.
L'Oreal	Because I'm worth it.
Morton Salt	When it rains, it pours.
Wheaties	Breakfast of champions.
Wendy's	Where's the beef?

Have you identified your point of differentiation yet? Remember this is the first step to improving your **VRIO** model! If you have identified your point of differentiation write it below:

Can you communicate this point of differentiation in a catchy tagline? This can be crucial in your promotional efforts – advertising, PR, special

events. See if you can come up with a word. What about a line like those listed in the exercise? Let your management team and employees contribute
ideas as well:

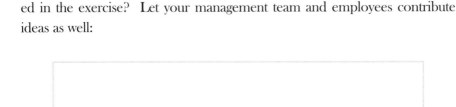

If you can summarize your differentiation in one line, you will have a
much greater chance of building on your differentiator. I often find people
who include too many concepts into an advertisement, postcard campaign or
newsletter, resulting in no single concept taking center stage. This is often the
reason that marketing campaigns fail. Sherwin Schwarz, producer of television
shows like *Gilligan's Island* and the *Brady Bunch,* when asked why all of his
television programs had theme songs that clearly outlined the premise of the
show, said, "That's easy...confused people don't buy." The more you can give
complete clarity on your product or service through a word or a phrase, the
more your clients will have an immediate recognition and opportunity to
engage with your brand.

I often meet people who want to change their messages frequently. They
get bored by saying the same thing over and over in their messaging. But
remember, it is repetition that helps cut through the clutter. Your clients will
not get bored with a repetitive message. We come to rely on those taglines
because they reinforce the brand promise. Some companies have been using
their taglines for more than thirty years! They know their customers won't get
bored with it because their customers – like yours – are getting bombarded
with thousands of messages a day from other companies. They need your
tagline to be consistent in order to remember you. If you have a good tagline,
don't change it. If you don't, start to work on one. Working with an advertising professional or a company that specializes in corporate brand and identity
can be a tremendous help in the development of a powerful tagline. Think of
it as an investment that you will use for many years to come.

What if my offering does not meet all the VRIO criteria?

You may be wondering if your company can survive if you haven't met all VRIO criteria. Dr. Barney has a simple way of viewing what your returns will be, based on your VRIO analysis.

VRIO Framework with Competitive and Economic Consequences

If your offering is

Valuable?	NO	YES	YES	YES
Rare?	-	NO	YES	YES
Costly to Imitate?	-	-	NO	YES
Organizationally Leveraged?	NO	NO	NO	YES
Competitive Implications	Competitive Disadvantage.	Competitive Parity.	Temporary Competitive Advantage.	Sustained Competitive Advantage.
Economic Performance	Below Average Returns.	Average Returns.	Above Average Returns.	Above Average Returns.

You have completed one of the most important exercises you will ever need thanks to Dr. Barney. Use this often as the market and your product will change over time.

Peter Drucker said "Because its purpose is to create a customer, the business has two – and only two – functions: marketing and innovation. Marketing and innovation create value, all the rest are costs." Branding is communicated through marketing and keeps its differentiation through innovation of products and services to meet the changing needs of the market. This chart will prompt you to achieve both in any company, in any market.

SECTION II:
35 Remarkable Companies Who Got It Right

CHAPTER 5
Brandstorming: Thirty-five Companies that Will Spark Your Imagination and Build Your Brand Quotient

"Formulate and stamp indelibly on your mind a mental picture
of yourself as succeeding. Hold this picture tenaciously.
Never permit it to fade. Your mind will seek to develop the picture.
Do not build up obstacles in your imagination."

—Norman Vincent Peale

You've undoubtedly been through brainstorming exercises where people call out ideas without restriction. The ideas are written on a tablet or board and ultimately narrowed down to a few select choices. Brandstorming works in very much the same way. By looking at how others have created brand identities, you can often find inspiration for your own company. I decided to use small and medium sized companies in the majority of the businesses outlined in this book to demonstrate that you don't have to be a Fortune 500 company to have a successful brand.

The companies below have incredible ideas for differentiation. We will go through the strategies of thirty five small and medium sized businesses. It's impossible to read these without feeling your own ideas bubbling to the top. Not every concept will apply to your company, but I'm a believer that creativity begets creativity. One idea can spark another. It's also inspirational to hear the stories of people who didn't have all the answers from the beginning. In most cases, these people went with their gut, changed their strategies when necessary, kept moving forward, and prevailed.

Each company will be introduced by its differentiation strategy. Woven throughout the story will be the tactics that helped carry out this strategy. At the end of each section, you will be asked to answer questions using the brandstorming process, to see how these strategies or tactics might apply to your company. Do this with an open mind and no boundaries – creativity cannot happen within boundaries. If thinking without limits gives you fearful thoughts like, "we'll never be able to afford this," or "that wouldn't fly in our industry," know this: once you allow yourself to be creative and even unrealistic, you will be able to hone in on the ideas and make them work for your company. You have to dream big, then scale it down to fit your budget, and your circumstances. Let creativity come first, practicality second. While this concept will make your operations and accounting people crazy, like it does at my company, we manage to take the lofty ideas and bring them down to the scale of the budget. This allows creation without restriction. If you feel limited by budget, you won't be in the right mindset for creativity.

Strategy# 1:

Change consumer buying habits in your favor

NETFLIX

Netflix - *www.netflix.com*

Is there anything more painful than walking into a video rental store? Last time I visited a national video chain store, it took me five minutes to find a parking space. When I entered the store, which was swarming with customers, I noticed that a toddler had pulled about forty DVDs from the rack, which were piled at her feet. The whole store seemed to be in a state of disarray. Many of the films I wanted were unavailable. When I finally did find one, I waited in a long line only to have the young clerk at the register tell me that my membership had expired. I filled out a new membership application which I gave to a different employee. She detached a thin strip of perforated paper from the bottom of the form, nearly tearing it in half, handed me the torn strip, and said, "Here. This is your contract." I showed it to the clerk who, before processing my order, said in a deadpan voice, "Miss Sellani, are you aware that you owe $6 in overdue charges from your last video rental?" I threw my "contract" in the trash on my way out, and never returned to the store again.

Fortunately for me and millions of DVD renters there is hope. There is Netflix. Netflix offers more than 65,000 film and TV titles that you can choose from the convenience of your computer (an average video store's selection is between two and three thousand). Most movies are mailed to you within a day and there are no due dates or late fees. When you return the movie in the prepaid red envelope, the next movie in your queue is shipped to you automatically for a membership fee as low as $10 per month.

With that type of offering, it's not surprising that Netflix has gained significant growth through word of mouth in its eight year history. Director of Corporate Communications Steve Swasey says, "more than 90 percent of Netflix members refer someone else to Netflix." By leveraging technology to provide convenience, selection and value, Netflix is changing the way Americans rent movies. And now, competitors are feeling the pain.

Swasey says, "In the San Francisco Bay area alone, Netflix market share has grown to more than 13 percent of households; at the same time, Blockbuster closed ten percent of its Bay area stores – there's a direct correlation." According to Hoover's, a D&B company, Netflix's 2005 net income increased by nearly 95 percent over the previous year, prompting competitive giants to change their strategies.

Blockbuster entered the online business after Netflix and reportedly has 1.5 million members at the time of this writing. "By the end of 2006, Netflix is scheduled to have more than 6 million," says Swasey. Netflix was ranked 36th of America's Top 2000 Brands in *Brandweek*'s article "Superbrands 2006." Blockbuster retail stores and online video stores placed respectively at 114 and 385. Swasey says, "Warren Buffet calls it 'building motes around the business' – creating a product that's difficult to imitate."

Despite the company's significant head start, Netflix relies on customer research to maintain the company's lead and keep the brand fresh and exciting. "Great branding companies listen to their clients," Swasey says. "We lead focus groups several times a week and send about one million daily email polls to track satisfaction and shipment time. We may be a technology company run by software engineers, but we're consumer friendly because we listen to our customers. Building a brand is not just about technology – it's about offering sustainable value. The graveyard is full of great technology that was never marketed."

This practice has ranked Netflix the number one website in the world for customer satisfaction three periods in a row, according to ForeSee Results and

FGI Researchers, independent research firms. Another factor in Netflix's success is the stability of its management team which has only changed by one member in more than six years due to retirement.

But success also breeds competition. Swasey says, "We like competition – we have to continue to be better. Customers don't care about our first mover advantage and patented processes - they care about the product."

And the product is improving in big ways. Netflix is filling in the gaps left behind by Hollywood's mass appeal model. "America's taste in movies is broad, vast and more diverse than the new releases that Hollywood puts out," Swasey says. "The 1.4 million shipments that Netflix sends out each day include documentaries, independent films in more than 200 genres," or, as Swasey jokes, "everything from yoga to Yoda."

Netflix is even helping filmmakers by giving movies that are relatively well known but unwatched in theaters a second chance to gain viewers. Almost as many people saw *Hotel Rwanda* through Netflix as in the theaters. Netflix is also acquiring exclusive rights to distribute original special interest movies which big theaters can't financially justify. Swasey explains, "Only about ten of the Sundance Film Festival's 2,000 film submissions end up with a distributor. There's an enormous body of talent with no distribution channel for their films." One such film is *Bituminous Coal Queens of Pennsylvania* produced by Patricia Heaton and her husband which didn't have a wide enough appeal for big screen audiences, but received a warm reception from Netflix members.

Through the company's steady growth, Swasey keeps a healthy and creative brand perspective. "If Netflix was a person, it would be a leader, an innovator, a friend, a motivator, and an exiting person to be around. We strive to make the brand like the person we want it to be."

Brandstorming Questions

1. Where is the pain in most transactions in my industry?
    a. Access to inventory?
    b. Customer service?
    c. Waiting time?
    d. Returns?
    e. Other?

2. How can I change my company's processes to remove the pain for my customers?

3. Am I utilizing research on every transaction to determine client satisfaction and preferences?

4. Am I conducting focus groups to determine shifts in buying preferences or opportunities that exist because of my competitor's weaknesses?

Differentiation Strategy # 2:

Brand a commodity

HEAROS - *www.hearos.com*

You might say that Doug Pick has an ear for business. While conducting feasibility analyses at USC's Entrepreneur Program, he identified the factors that make a market suitable for entry - factors like low barriers to entry and lack of brand name dominance in the retail peg space. With that in mind, he identified an opportunity that met these criteria. The result was the transformation of a commodity into a successful and exciting brand - earplugs.

Not very exciting, you say? What if I told you that Pick has reported selling 12 million pair in 2006? If you're not hearing a beautiful "cha-ching" sound, then maybe you need to have your ears examined.

Pick, founder of the **HEAROS** brand, further describes the offering, "the product is disposable and highly consumable. People use, lose, and purchase them over and over again – like socks. And the market's never going to go away." People will always need to protect their hearing from water or noise.

"What was appealing to me was the fact that I could sell to drug stores, music stores, motorcycle stores, college book stores, and health shops. With multiple markets, I could diversify my start up risks."

But as a rising entrepreneur, earning credibility with retailers would take time. "It took me four years to land Walgreens, eight to get Wal-Mart, nine to get Target, twelve to get Kmart and fourteen to get Rite Aid," says Pick.

"The big box retailers can take your business into the stratosphere." And they did. While on the way, he relied on smaller retail accounts which enabled him not only to grow the business and stay profitable, but to try unique branding tactics within niche vertical markets.

"I was in a market where no attention had been paid to packaging, marketing, promotion, or publicity. The opportunity was clearly there. The competition wasn't doing anything." He remembered the words of his grandfather who said, "sell the sizzle not the steak – but you better have a good steak."

So Pick made a great steak. Relying again on solid research and gut instincts he knew that earplugs were not a destination purchase. "They're not something people put on their grocery list. Most often, it's an impulse purchase – when people see them, they buy them. That's why the packaging should be as dynamic as possible. In retail you have a millisecond to attract someone's eyes and to have that firecracker go off in their head – 'my husband snores' or 'I'm going to a concert.'"

So he created brightly colored packaging, promotions, publicity and television campaigns to make **HEAROS** stand out amidst the sea of earplugs offered by competitors. "How will you use HEAROS?" is the question posed on his website (*www.hearos.com*). With answers to the question under colorful icons - Music, Sleep, Water, Travel, Auto Races, Firearms, Study, Loud Noises. He added clever names for each product like "Rock and Roll," "High Fidelity" and "Sleep Pretty in Pink."

"We're light years ahead of the competition" says Pick. "We use advertising, publicity and promotions. I also treat the retailer like a partner. We're doing what we can to drive traffic to the retailers and boost their bottom line."

And that means using sound judgment about the product he delivers to retailers. "I won't get involved with distributing a product if I don't feel it works." What's worked to date is Pick's ability to capitalize on competitive weaknesses. "Everything we offer is the antithesis of what previously existed – we flipped the equation of what it is to market an earplug." And in doing so, he transformed a bland commodity into a profitable brand. And what entrepreneur wouldn't love the sound of that?

Brandstorming Questions

1. Is my industry a commodity in the mind of my customers?

2. Does my company look like my competitors and claim to do the same thing everyone else does, only better?

3. From my consumer's perspective is there really a difference in my offering? How do I know?

4. How can I create an experience that can never be associated with a commodity service?

Strategy # 3:

Create a brand personality

Strategy #4:

Create an industry standard in your favor

The Supporting Cast -
www.supportingcast.com

Anserteam -
www.anserteam.com

What do you do if the very mention of your industry evokes immediate feelings of negativity or distrust? Give it a great personality. That's what Phil Jakeway did. As President of The Supporting Cast, he personified his brand in a way that gives prospects something to smile about every time they receive a cold call from his, uh, employment agency.

The term employment agency or the slightly less off-putting "staffing firm" still sends a chill down the collective spines of human resources managers everywhere, often bringing to mind endless cold calls from countless firms, all of whom claim to have the best candidate for your needs. They all have "the best temps." They all have "the best permanent candidates." They all have "the most experienced recruiters in the industry."

"By definition, that can't be true," says Jakeway. "We've been in business for eighteen years and we really do have excellent temp and perm applicants and recruiters who really are among the best in the business - but if the 300+ staffing firms in NYC are all making that same claim, it's extremely difficult to differentiate yourself in the mind of the consumer."

Jakeway's brand sets the stage for a positive reception from prospects while leveraging the theatrical verve of the company's New York City base. Getting a call from "The Supporting Cast" sounds friendlier and more intriguing than a call from "ABC Staffing." The name can make a huge difference.

His web site and collateral materials also stay true to the theme, calling their recruiters "talent scouts." The strategy has kept his business thriving for nearly two decades, but most of that business was initially with local companies. Jakeway knew there was more than local business out there - business that would require yet another strategy for this one-city act. So he prepared for Scene II of a branding strategy that would put his company before a national audience.

"As an independent agency in a single city, we realized we didn't have the name recognition of national staffing firms. But I learned that in a great majority of the areas around the country, those national companies did not do a good job of delivering quality staffing services."

Jakeway's research revealed that the majority of independent firms had higher conversion rates of temporary to permanent staff than their national counterparts. In other words, the smaller, independent firms were better at selecting the right people – people for the temporary assignment that their clients ultimately wanted to keep as permanent employees.

Three years ago, Jakeway developed a new strategy along with two other independent staffing firm leaders - Valerie Freeman from Dallas based Imprimis (*www.imprimis.com*) and Sue Romanos from Miami based Career Exchange (*www.careerexchange.com*). Jakeway recalls, "We saw an opportunity to form an alliance of independent staffing services across the country. It would enable us to go to national companies and explain that we can provide a higher quality of service than national firms."

They started by trademarking the alliance with another memorable name – ANSERTEAM (The Alliance of National Staffing and Employment Resources). But like The Supporting Cast, ANSERTEAM is more than just a clever name. The alliance upholds the highest standards for those who join, creates barriers to entry for the competition and ensures quality services to their clients. Every firm that joins gets an exclusive geographic market territory and must be recommended to the alliance for consideration. Each applicant goes through a rigorous application and screening process, reference checks, and a review of business practices. Members must agree to uphold the quality and best practices of ANSERTEAM. The alliance's offering to clients includes a quality versus quantity approach (attacking the weaknesses of the national high volume model), diversity initiatives, efficiencies that result in greater return on investment and cutting edge technology that streamlines the hiring process, reduces billing errors, and delivers reports on-demand.

"The national firms sell themselves on low pricing and rely on volume for their profit," says Jakeway. But by choosing a differentiation rather than a low-cost strategy, his firm will never need to rely on low commodity pricing. Offering a valuable service and geographic exclusivity, ANSERTEAM empowers its members to differentiate themselves from local independents and to compete with national players. For example, The Supporting Cast is now the only independent staffing firm in all of New York City to have the ANSERTEAM designation – an instant differentiator. On the national front, they can also compete by letting companies know that, through the ANSERTEAM alliance, they have access to quality independent staffing companies with a higher level of industry standards in every major U.S. Market.

And ANSERTEAM can back up these claims with powerful numbers. After only three years in existence, they now operate in 228 branches throughout the US, with each member organization having an average of twenty-five years in the industry. In 2005, they serviced 30,000 clients, making more than 160,000 placements for a total of nearly $823 million in annual revenue. Powerful claims that couldn't be made by any of its individual members now become a part of each member's respective positioning strategies.

The alliance enabled The Supporting Cast to return to the stage with a brand new story – or, perhaps, a new brand story. "We had been trying to do business with one of the largest medical insurance companies on the East Coast for nearly a year" said Jakeway. "Their typical response to us was 'we get calls like this all the time – we don't have time to meet with you.'" This is an understandable response in an industry where everyone looks alike. When The ANSERTEAM concept was included in the Supporting Cast's phone pitch, the same insurer had a sudden change of heart – and found the time for a meeting. Fifteen minutes into the meeting, the company agreed to work with The Supporting Cast in the NYC market and is considering using them in national markets as well.

The Supporting Cast now has a difference worthy of a standing ovation in both name and offering, opening doors to business opportunities locally and nationwide.

Other Great Company Names that Reflect Brand Personality

Bark, Bath and Beyond
Pet Boutique and Bakery
Laguna Beach, CA
www.barkbathandbeyond.com

Curl Up N Dye
Hair Salon
Las Vegas, NV
www.curlupndye.com

Franks for the Memories
Sidewalk Café featuring unforgettable hot dogs
Buena Vista, Virginia
www.franks4thememories.com

Groomingdale's
Pet Grooming Services
Winston-Salem, NC
www.groomingdales.com

Schooner or Later
Waterfront Restaurant
Long Beach, CA
www.schoonerorlater.com

Sprinkles
Cupcake Bakery
Beverly Hills & Newport Beach, CA
www.sprinklescupcakes.com

Sweeping Beauty
Housekeeping Service
San Diego, CA
http://www.servicemagic.com/rated.SleepingBeauty.8257908.html

The FURminator
Dog de-shedding tool
St. Louis, MO
www.furminator.com

Yam Good Pies
Sweet Potato Pie Bakery
Lagrange, GA

Wok Around the Clock
Chinese Restaurant
Earlville, Queensland, Australia

Brandstorming Questions

1. What does my company's name say about the personality of my brand?

2. Does my name accurately convey what the company represents?

3. Is it easy for others to know what your company does by the name?

4. Does my company excel at any industry standard? If so, can this be used as a point of differentiation?

5. Can I create an organized membership group that would position me and its other members as experts in our field?

6. What other measures can I take to position myself as an expert in a way that my competition cannot?

Strategy # 5:

Give it away for free

free realtime.com

Freerealtime.com - *www.freerealtime.com*

How does a powerful brand survive one of the darkest times in an industry's history? Ask Michael Neufeld, who lived to tell of the rise and fall and rise again of a dot-com brand that first began by giving it all away.

Neufeld remembers the early days when his company, like legions of other dot-comers, had a powerful idea and plenty of zealous investors to fund it. The internet frenzy was the backdrop for FreeRealTime which began in 1998 with a noble and ambitious goal: to level the playing field for the individual investor by being the first player on the web to provide unlimited, free, real-time stock quotes to the masses.

According to Neufeld, "the company's goal was to empower the general public – it was good for the investor and good for the stock market. We wanted to give individual investors the same real-time market information only available to professional traders - for free." And so they did.

Just ten years ago, the only people who had access to real time stock quotes were primarily stockbrokers, money managers and professional traders. Most individual investors either had no access to such data or, at best, could get a limited number of real time quotes online each month through their brokers as long as they actively traded and paid high commissions. They could choose from a few expensive subscription-based quote services available at the time. The only free market data available to the masses was delayed

15-20 minutes – an unacceptable offering, which essentially left investors to buy and sell with dated information in a market that was moving in real-time. All of that was about to change as FreeRealTime entered the market – with a branded URL that couldn't help but be picked up by search engines as eager traders began looking for "free real-time stock quotes." Success came suddenly.

"We spent hundreds of thousands of dollars each month on real-time market data, bandwidth, and other related costs, and in turn gave these quotes away for free," according to Neufeld. "Our revenues came primarily from advertisers," who were all too willing to have access to FreeRealTime's rapidly growing viewer base, "and, to a lesser degree, from subscribers of some of our high-end products." Competing companies offered a variety of financial content, which sometimes included real-time stock quotes on a paid subscription basis as well as stock research reports, investing commentary, and free delayed stock quotes – an inferior set of data.

FreeRealTime's management team felt the most valuable piece of information any investor needed to make effective trading decisions was the real-time quote – and they should be able to get it for free. They held this differentiator for quite some time and as a result, their audience exploded as website traffic soared. Further enhancing their credibility was the fact that FreeRealTime was never in the trading business and, as such, received no money for trades, unlike the online stock brokerages such as Ameritrade and ETrade. They were an unbiased, independent, financial news media company, and still are to this day. The business model brought the company to its highest point at 300 million page views per month, and 100,000 unique visitors per day – without a penny spent on their own advertising. For much of their history, they were named one of the most frequented financial websites, amongst formidable competitors like The Motley Fool at *www.fool.com* and *www.cbsmarketwatch.com*. They also were referred to as the "stickiest" e-finance site, sticky referring to the amount of time a person spends daily on a particular website. This was of particular interest to the advertising community – FreeRealTime's bread and butter.

As was common in the days of the dot-com frenzy, internet investors were paying for growth, not profitability. And FreeRealTime did grow, with an eye toward increasing profits. But in the great tradition of early dot-coms, the company lost millions of dollars in executing their business model – however, each sequential quarter was better than the last in the march toward profitability. When there were signs that the Internet space was beginning to crumble in 2000, the company began aggressively cutting costs and looking for new revenue streams. As a result, the model became more efficient and reached profitability and positive cash flow, but it wasn't enough to stave off the ill effects of the crash of 2000. The company that had empowered millions of stock enthusiasts and equipped them with the information to turn knowledge into wealth faced a crisis point.

"Fueling the dot-com crash was the slashing of online marketing and advertising budgets everywhere; our advertising revenue dropped by 90 percent almost overnight," according to Neufeld. "During our growth period, we had added considerable headcount and related costs, both through internal growth as well as through acquisition of synergistic companies, including an independent stock research firm." To keep the company alive, the company laid off personnel, downsized the entire organization, sold previously acquired businesses, in order to scale down while still keeping the core business model intact. Neufeld says, "We divested ourselves of everything ancillary while the industry reinvented itself, and remained in the space that we pioneered. We embarked on a reorganization and turnaround while other companies fell by the wayside."

FreeRealTime was one of only a few formerly public dot-coms that filed and emerged from a Chapter 11 reorganization still standing today as a private enterprise. The management team that stayed through this process accomplished this reorganization without any external financing, working for no salaries in some cases. Through cost reduction, remodeling of business revenue streams, and armed with a powerful brand with a loyal following, the company was able to persevere and retain a significant customer base – many of whom were now willing to pay a small monthly subscription price to save the company that empowered them with free real-time market data for all of those years.

"We migrated thousands of people to the paid subscription model," said Neufeld, "where they receive unlimited real-time quotes, and a variety of investment information and premium content, including personalized email alerts and updates about their stock investments. Our new subscription products, joined with a rejuvenated advertising marketplace, have resulted in a more balanced revenue model for the company as we sit here today."

For a $10 monthly fee, viewers can now purchase a product called FRT Express, which enables them to track their favorite stocks in real-time, using watch lists, charts, stock alerts, and other valuable tools. The system provides both information and an inherent barrier to exit – most people don't want to stop subscribing because it's a simple product and contains so much personalized data, it would require a significant amount of time to start over with a competitive product. FreeRealTime still maintains its status as an independent source of information, not tied to commissions on trades, which gives users a comfort level they may not experience with other providers. They also provide a variety of higher end streaming-quote products, but have stayed true to their brand model of giving the basic information at an affordable price to enable their customers to build wealth.

"We don't succumb to every expensive cool new product that comes our way. Although we offer premium high-end trading tools and content to those willing to pay a higher price, say $50 each month, I believe that most people want a certain amount of basic and reliable real-time information to make good investment decisions – that's the only curve you need to stay ahead of. We'll stick primarily to those basic offerings and keep it in the $10-$15/month range so that we appeal to the majority of investors out there. However, we will not alienate anybody as we offer an arsenal of trading tools that appeal to the most sophisticated investor."

By staying true to the original brand promise of empowering the everyday, individual investor, they were able to migrate thousands of their previously "free" customers into "paying" customers, and thus survive the industry downturn with the help of a fiercely loyal customer base. "Our company was a pioneer in helping individual investors, who in turn, paid us back with their loyal support. Some called us heroes because of what we did" says Neufeld.

Although the dot-com crash almost put the company out of business like it did to so many others, FreeRealTime is a dot-com survivor of the rarest breed. Employing a cost reduction and consolidation strategy through a Chapter 11 reorganization, which included reducing a staff of 150 employees to a bare minimum of eight, and divestiture of cash guzzling acquisitions, as well as converting thousands of loyal free content users to paying subscribers, the company turned itself around and has flourished. FreeRealTime emerged from Chapter 11 in the spring of 2003, modeling perseverance through the most challenging of times. Brand loyalty can only come through promises kept. And when FreeRealTime.com was no longer able to give everything away for free and survive, customers who gained wealth from this business model are now happy to give something back in return.

Brandstorming Questions

1. What if any advantages can my company obtain by giving a product or service away for free? *(Note – this is a long term strategy – not a one week special "free" deal)*

2. If I could obtain new clients because of a free service, what complementary for-profit services or products could I provide?

3. Is a subscription based model for a product or service something that my company can consider?

Strategy # 6:

Trademark a powerful tagline, then live it

The Business Generator - *www.klymshyn.com*

You won't find John Klymshyn backing prospects into a corner with a canned sales pitch, strong-arming them with a barrage of features and benefits, or intimidating them with a high-pressure close. His kinder, gentler approach to transactions is a clear departure from the traditional sales training methods which cause most of us to run the other way when in the path of an oncoming peddler. When I read his book *Move the Sale Forward,* my immediate impression was, "he's put the humanity back into sales." And in doing so, he created a valuable product for sales people and a strong brand differentiator for himself.

According to the Direct Selling Association (*www.dsa.org*), there are approximately 13.6 million salespeople in the United States. It's no wonder that a Google search for "sales trainers" yields more than 9 million results. So how has Klymshyn endured for more than two decades amidst legions of competitors? By developing a strategy that addresses the core of sales failures and referencing that strategy with a memorable tagline that he leverages throughout every element of his business.

People who have difficulty selling often fear two things –cold calling and dealing with rejection. And who wouldn't? John has minimized the fear factor by a concept he calls "Moving Conversations Forward," a trademarked tagline and a slight variation from his book title.

This phrase resonates with sales people as human beings first and sales people second, suddenly diminishing the anxiety of the selling process. After all, what sales person is afraid of a little conversation? And if the conversation eliminates the "hard sell", how can a prospective client be suspicious of one?

John's philosophies are in direct opposition to traditional sales training norms. In his book he states, "Your goal should not be the closing of the sale. Your goal should not be to make more money either. These goals will leave you short of the ultimate goal: finding those people with whom you can truly connect, and as a result, conduct effective business."

This simple philosophy makes the sales process more enjoyable for both the salesperson and the prospect. John also teaches practical methods of discipline with his Twenty Call Burst and Open Ended Killer Questions, all designed to – you guessed it – move the conversation forward. His methods don't always result in closing the deal – and that's okay – they're not intended to.

John replaces traditional closing statements like "I'll call you next week" with a question to the client, "When should we talk again?" the latter allowing input from the prospect. Similarly another common sales pitch, "I'd like to come to your office to show you..." is replaced by "what do you think our next step should be?" These types of questions suddenly take the prospect out of the defensive position into a partnership role. By rejecting antiquated selling practices, John focuses on the human connection. And, as a person who has been on the prospect end of John's conversations, I can assure you, it's a powerful process. I've hired John to speak at my own company to an audience of more than 500 salespeople. I never felt pressured by him, but we both arrived at the same conclusion – that we needed to move the conversation forward. And in doing so, a business arrangement seemed like the right idea for both of us.

John's trademarked statement is leveraged throughout his business which includes keynote speeches, seminars, workshops and one-to-one coaching. Even his answering machine messages states, "thank you for calling – I look forward to moving our conversation forward." In the last nine years, John's business has flourished and he continues to keep his familiar tagline. His consistency enables him to cut through the clutter of countless competitors.

One of the most common mistakes I see in business is a change of the tagline or other creative element because the company president, marketing department or sales team gets tired of it. Big mistake. A wise Southern California attorney named Steve Sunshine once told me, that effective communication doesn't happen by saying 100 different things one time, it happens by saying one thing 100 different times. I constantly remind business leaders that they will get bored with their phrase, concept or tagline long before anyone else will. Keep using it. Consumers don't want you to change. They want to know what to expect. John always lets his clients know and he consistently delivers.

More On Great Taglines

A tagline is a compelling one liner, which, if done well, can convey your company's differentiation in a single memorable sentence. Taglines are important for two reasons – since most consumers will tune you out in a matter of seconds, if you can convey your value proposition quickly, you might have a chance at getting their business. But a second good reason to create a tagline is for you. If you can summarize your company in a memorable and compelling way, giving clients and prospects an understanding of your primary brand differentiator you will be able to communicate it effectively in all of your messaging. Taglines should be clever, humorous or compelling, and always memorable.

Finally, taglines are not just for the big companies. Anyone can have a great tagline, so get creative and find one you can love and live with for many years to come.

These are a few of my favorite taglines – even though some of them are no longer in use, they are still memorable to me. That's the power of a great tagline.

My Favorite Taglines

"You leave 'em, we'll love 'em."
Dog Day Care Center
Newport Beach, CA

"We teach people the skills you thought they had when you hired them."
Business Training Works
Port Tobacco, MD
www.businesstrainingworks.com

"Sit. Stay."
Animal Planet Television
www.animalplanet.com

"Mm, mm, mm, mm, mm. Toasty."
Quizno's Subs
Denver, CO
www.quiznos.com

"The Pfabuluous Pfaucet with the Pfunny name."
        And
"Phreshest ideas in phaucets."
Pfister Faucets
Lake Forest, CA
www.pricepfister.com

Brandstorming Questions

1. Does my company have a tagline or slogan?

2. Does my tagline or slogan succinctly and clearly state my point of differentiation without needing additional explanation?

3. Am I leveraging my tagline by using it on all marketing materials?

4. Am I ensuring that my company exemplifies my tagline or differentiation in everything we do?

Strategy # 7:

Be relentlessly old-fashioned

Victory Pig Pizza

The Victory Pig Pizza parlor doesn't have a website, a chat room or a blog. They don't blast email coupons to their customers. In fact, they don't even advertise. They only open their doors for business three days a week from 4:30 p.m. to 11:00 p.m. And they like it that way. Owner Rich Ceccoli says, "If you have a good product, the customers will come when you're open." And they do. Because Victory Pig Pizza is a slice of pure nostalgic bliss.

Being relentlessly old-fashioned has paid off for the company that has been in business in a small Northeastern Pennsylvania suburb since 1942. Its unusual name combines a reference to the victory of World War II and their famous **BBQ** pork sandwiches. But the menu item that keeps people coming back for more is the pizza, and an old-fashioned way of doing business which creates impeccable consistency in both product and service.

Just ask 71-year old bartender Joe who has been serving drinks there for 56 years. Or waitress Dorothy who recently retired after 62 years of service. You can also check with kitchen manager Paul, who started working at the restaurant when he was a sophomore in high school – he's now 52 years old. But they're all just rookies compared to Lisa, the 94 year-old kitchen worker who recently left her post after a hip fracture. She wants to return however. She misses the bustling 700 square foot kitchen with temperatures that never drop below 110 degrees Fahrenheit. All of these faithful employees can tell you that the secret of Victory Pig's success is their relentless adherence to an old-fashioned recipe and process, and a refusal to change with the whims of modern times.

Even more impressive than their employee retention program, is the Victory Pig's family recipe and procedures known only to Ceccoli and his father. Ceccoli's parents, Robert and Mary Ceccoli are still very much a part of the organization ensuring that the kitchen produces the authentic taste for which Victory Pig is known. Both are 81 years old and never miss a day at the restaurant. Up until three years ago, they were even using the same ovens that started the culinary magic in 1942. When Ceccoli finally broke down and purchased new ovens, they were immediately taken apart and reassembled to meet his specific needs. Ceccoli recalls, "My dad did most of the alterations on the new ovens as my grandfather taught him many years ago. Of course I watched and helped so I would know for the future." Like the recipe, the oven reassembly is a trade secret that has enabled Ceccoli to continue the special process which bakes every sumptuous slice to an old-fashioned Victory Pig perfection.

Old fashioned also means a meticulous rigidity for details and systems. Every day 700 pounds of dough are purchased. Tomatoes are crushed by hand. Fresh Bermuda onions are thinly sliced. All this is done in the morning hours, so pizza can be made fresh when the guests arrive at 4:30 p.m. And the word "reheat" is simply not a part of the Victory Pig vernacular. "Each person gets a hot fresh pizza every time," says Ceccoli. "This is the real secret to our success."

The process begins when a full cup of oil is poured into each pizza pan, followed by a layer of dough, which is dressed with crushed tomatoes, Bermuda onions and one slice of cheese per serving. It takes up to three months to teach a rookie to spin up to eight pans at a time to create the remarkably consistent product. The pizza pans are placed exactly ¼ inch apart - any more and the product would burn. The pans are placed into ovens so hot (even the temperature is a secret), that the pizza doesn't bake in its bed of oil– it fries. What about cholesterol and carbs? Fuhgeddaboudit. When you're doing things the old fashioned way, there's no room for Dr. Atkins or

South Beach.

Once removed from the ovens, the pizza is served on those thin paper plates that your mother used at family picnics. Your first reaction is to marvel at the steaming hot rectangular wedge as it seeps oil into the absorbent dish. The aroma fills the dining room. And then, it happens. You bite into a mouthful of this heavenly, calorie-laden wonderment, which is hot and crunchy on the bottom and velvety soft on top. The thinly sliced onions are placed below the surface of the cheese, which clings to the roof of your mouth, allowing you to savor it just a bit longer. And it's then you realize, this old-fashioned thing – it works.

The twenty - table diner serves only a portion of their audience of eager eaters. The curb service, another nostalgic element, accommodates an additional 120 cars. Phone orders bring the total of people served up to 800-1000 nightly. Not bad for a staff of thirty part-time employees.

In today's warp speed world, keeping it old-school is a scary thing to do. Ceccoli says that because they have chosen not to advertise, Victory Pig is missing out on the growing number of teens in the area who eat, God forbid, pizza from chain stores. But his old-fashioned ingenuity has even found a way around that.

Ceccoli also owns a miniature golf course located behind the restaurant. When teen parties and dances are held at the golf course, he is all too happy to supply free mini-slices of pizza to ravenous youngsters in a perpetual search of free food. They love it. They want more. They ask where they can get it. "Just three feet away," is the answer - and a new generation of customers is born.

And, even with an old-school charm, there is still room for expansion – as long as consistency rules. Ceccoli says, "I am now working on a way to preserve our dough. If I can do so we may be able to expand Victory Pig to more than one store but all the ingredients would be prepared at our mother store."

For now, they'll settle for nothing but the best product for their customers. If Victory Pig runs out of ingredients before 11:00 p.m., they politely apologize before turning customers away. It's a hard thing to do, but that's the way it is when you have a meticulous regard for perfection - there is simply no room for compromise. And if that's old fashioned, pass me another slice.

Victory Pig before

Victory Pig today

Brandstorming Questions

1. What traditionally old-fashioned elements could make my business stand out from the competition? This can be as simple as hand written thank you notes or as detailed as a customer care plan. Some traditional customer service items:
   a. Sending gifts to clients.
   b. A phone call from a prominent person in the company.
   c. Remembering customers by name.
   d. Creating unforgettable experiences – these do not have to be expensive.
   e. Not following every new fad – staying the course.
   f. Consistent handling of customers so that they know what to expect.

2. What secret or proprietary methods do I have that will give me a competitive advantage? How will I leverage these? Include secret processes, recipes, or methods.

3. Does high employee turnover impact my ability to provide a con sistent product or quality services? How can I turn this around?

Strategy # 8:

Change the business model

Sperry Van Ness - *www.svn.com*

Otto von Bismarck, Founder and Chancellor of the German Empire in the late 1800's said that to gain respect for sausages and laws, you shouldn't watch either being made. I'd like to add a third item to Otto's list – commercial real estate transactions.

You're about to learn one of the industry's dirty little secrets from someone who learned about it the hard way. But it won't be a secret for long because Sperry Van Ness is telling the world about it. And the truth is a powerful differentiator in an industry of secrets.

As a new agent with Sperry Van Ness Commercial Real Estate, I was working on an apartment deal back in 1998 when I found two apartments listed by two separate outside brokerage firms. Both properties were perfect for my client, who had a significant amount of money, excellent credit and motivation to act immediately on the purchase.

I called each listing agent on behalf of my buyer and asked each of them to send me information on their listings. Both agents assured me they would send packages in the mail (this was before the Internet was the primary vehicle for sending property information). I anxiously waited for the packages to arrive – two days, three days, ten days. I finally said to my sales manager, "What are the odds that both packages would get lost in the mail?" He laughed out loud. He already knew the secret that I was about to learn. He said, "They didn't get lost! These guys don't want to work with you!" I said naively, "Why not? I have a qualified buyer for their property!" He said, "So what. They don't want your buyer because they're going to have to pay you for bringing him to the table– they'll find their own buyers and "double-end" the deal" (keep the entire commission for themselves). Double ending itself isn't a bad thing – if the listing agent also brings the highest bidder to the table. But an agent can never know if he has the highest bidder until he invites *all* bidders to compete.

I couldn't fathom that any agent would turn away a qualified bidder on their listing. My client might have been the top bidder, but no one will ever know. Both properties sold without his offer ever being seen by the seller and I learned a valuable lesson. If you're selling a property using a traditional brokerage firm, there's a good chance your listing agent is keeping bidders away by turning them down directly or by not marketing the property to them in the first place. I would later find industry statistics to support this claim.

This is not an isolated incident. It's how commercial real estate is sold every day – in relative secrecy and with little or no cooperation among brokerage firms. And guess who loses? The person who sells the property. They will never know how many buyers never got to bid on their property because their own listing agent wouldn't allow it.

When Sperry Van Ness created a business model which included aggressively marketing every property to the entire brokerage community – including their own competitors, cooperating with all brokers who represented buyers and sharing their commissions 50/50 with the broker who ultimately brought a buyer to the deal, they weren't thinking about branding or differentiation. They were just doing what was best for the client.

Your understanding of this concept can save you hundreds of thousands of dollars when you are selling a commercial property or if you are selling residential property with an unenlightened agent. But the majority of residential agents sell properties they way they should be sold.

The first thing they do after listing your home is put it onto a database called the MLS (Multiple Listing Service). This lets all other brokers know that your property is for sale, so that they can bring their buyers to the table. Your agent then advertises the property in the newspaper and hosts an open house. They send out "Just Listed" postcards and they make sure the property is promoted on the web. By the time your agent is done marketing your home, every buyer and broker knows about it. And that's the way it should be.

By marketing the property to potential buyers, and the brokers who represent them, the home will sell for true market value. Because true market value is whatever the highest bidder is willing to pay. When the transaction is completed, the listing agent will share the commission with the buyer's agent. This commission serves as an incentive for all brokers to bring their best buyers to the table. When a different brokerage firm represents the buyer and the seller, the deal is said to be co-brokered. On average, co-brokered deals sell at a higher sales price than those that are not co-brokered.

In contrast, commercial properties are sold in relative secrecy, to the significant detriment of the seller. What's worse is that most property owners don't have a clue that they are losing significant amounts of money when they sell their commercial properties and until they understand what I'm about to tell you, they'll keep losing money. Get ready for the facts.

Eighty percent of the time in the U.S., commercial properties are sold without being "co-brokered." But as I said earlier, co-brokered properties tend to sell at a higher price – so why wouldn't a broker cooperate? The reason the properties are not co-brokered is because most commercial property buyers and their brokers never know the property is on the market in the first place.

If you have ever sold a commercial property, it is statistically likely that your agent would show the property to few buyers that he knows personally. He would sell your property and keep the full commission because he represented both sides of the deal. He'll tell you there's no need to market the property because he knows the most likely buyer. You sell the property – maybe even at a profit. So what's wrong with this process? Your listing agent failed to do one vitally important thing. He didn't market the property to all prospective buyers and brokers and thus eliminated competition on your property.

Competition is what makes your property value increase. Competition is why co-brokered deals sell for more. If you have one bidder on your property, you can sell it. If you have ten bidders, you can sell if for more. So in the first scenario, you may make $500K profit, but you could have made $600K or $800K or more if the property had been marketed correctly. It's not rocket science. It's the simple law of supply and demand. But most commercial brokerage firms operate as if they are above the law.

To be fair, your commercial broker didn't put your listing on the MLS because there is no exclusive national MLS for commercial properties. But if there was, a traditional commercial broker would not likely use it because they would risk losing half their commission and it's simply not how the traditional industry model works. Most likely, your broker didn't let his competitors know about it. Chances are, he didn't even let the guy sitting next to him in his own office know about it. He only marketed to his own personal contacts. By excluding competition, he prevented all prospective buyers from bidding on the property and therefore, jeopardized your ability to get the maximum sales price. In some cases, like in my story above, he may not even have responded to brokers who had buyers, refusing to send information or return phone calls.

Still skeptical? Of course you are! Because you know I'm the VP of Marketing for Sperry Van Ness (or at least you know if you read my bio). You think I'm biased. You think I'm using this book to promote my company. Or perhaps you think I'm just another marketing scam artist. And since I had a feeling you'd be skeptical, I'm going to offer some objective third party data so that you can see if my outrageous claim that only 20 percent of commercial deals on average are co-brokered is true. Let's look at the Chicago market:

Chicago Office and Industrial Property Sales 2005
Source: CoStar COMPs (*www.CoStar.com*)

# of Deals	141	87	51
Average Sales Price	$12,099,981	$17,701,200	$28,100,000
# of Deals Where Listing Firm Cooperated with Buyers Firm	5	2	1
Percentage Co-brokered	3.5%	2.3%	2%
Percentage Double-Ended	96.5%	97.7%	98%

Of 141 office and industrial properties sold in Chicago in 2005, only five of them (3.5 percent) were co-brokered. Eighty seven deals only had 2.3 percent broker cooperation and fifty-one had 2 percent broker cooperation. It's not hard to understand why brokers in Chicago double end deals as much as 98 percent of the time – they get to keep the entire commission! And did you see the average prices? That's a big chunk of change. Who wouldn't want to keep it all? But what about the property owners? If the property was marketed to everyone, there would have been more bidders on the property; more bidders increase the likelihood of a higher sales price.

Many of the people who owned these properties thought they got a great deal. Because they sold in 2005, during one of the best periods in real estate history, they sold at a significant profit. What they don't know is they could have achieved an even greater return had their brokers marketed their listings to all prospective buyers. Brokers will actually prevent people from bidding on their own listings so they can double end deals even if it means the client will get less money.

Still not convinced? Look at Sperry Van Ness's numbers. Over the same time period as the deals listed above, Sperry Van Ness closed $9.5 billion in property sales – 70 percent of the time, Sperry Van Ness co-brokered the deal with an outside broker. In contrast, national competitors on average only co-brokered 20 percent of their deals.

Seem strange? It should. Especially when you consider the fact that largest five brokerage firms in the US only account for a 13 percent share of the entire market – so even the largest firms only have a relationship with a few percent points of the entire market. That in and of itself is not a problem – if they all shared their listings and their fees with every broker in the market. But since they don't, they are claiming to have the best buyer for the property in as many as 80 percent of the transactions when they only have few percentage points of the market. A mathematical impossibility!

In contrast, 70 percent of Sperry Van Ness deals are co-brokered and Sperry Van Ness gives half of the commission they negotiated to their own competitors! Those are some crazy do-gooders at Sperry Van Ness. Or are they? It depends. If you are motivated only by money, it is a crazy business model. If you want to do what's in the client's best interest, it's the only business model. In the last five years alone, Sperry Van Ness has given $100 million to their own competitors for bringing the highest bidder to the table – because that was in the client's best interest. And something crazy happens when you do right by your clients. You end up being a profitable company anyway.

When Rand Sperry and Mark Van Ness started this model of cooperation and compensation with outside brokers, they did it because they were tired of the lack of cooperation in the industry and the complete disregard for the client's return on investment. They founded the company certain that every competitor would copy their co-brokerage and commission sharing model. But no one did. Twenty years later, traditional firms are still selling properties the old fashioned way and unless commercial investors are wise, they're leaving large amounts of money on the table. And that's a shame.

Let's see how Sperry Van Ness sells the same property. Sperry Van Ness takes your listing and immediately starts marketing the property to prospective buyers and to more than 65,000 brokers who represent even more buyers. They conduct e-mail blasts, postcard campaigns, and create a property website. They invite competitors to view their new listings at monthly broker forums and let them know that they will co-broker the deal and share their commission 50/50. Sperry Van Ness gets not one, not two, but as much as twenty or more bids in some cases from people who are competing with each other to purchase the property. The seller can be assured that the highest bidder got that deal by competing with all other bids.

Need more proof? How about this? It's one of many testimonials where Sperry Van Ness had actually taken over a listing from other brokers who didn't find buyers for the property (because they weren't marketing it). The property sat on the market for two years before Sperry Van Ness took over the listing. By simply marketing to all brokers and investors, the Sperry Van Ness method created dramatic results:

> We had our building in Palos Heights, Illinois listed for sale with a local brokerage firm for over two years. The last year was spent with the building under contract but we were unsuccessful in finalizing a sale. We then listed with Sperry Van Ness. After spending a short period of time repositioning the building and implementing a marketing program we received a number of offers to purchase the property. The interest continued to escalate to the point that we had multiple qualified buyers submitting and resubmitting fully drafted purchase contracts at prices that moved higher and higher. We eventually accepted the best offer, one that was $200,000 higher than our original expectations. I believe Sperry Van Ness' proactive marketing program, which reaches many hundreds of key brokers and investors, was very instrumental in our ultimate success in the sale of this building. (Gerald M O'Grady, President, High Technology, Inc.)

Let's face it – the traditional model of commercial real estate is structured to give brokers an incentive to "sell" not to "maximize" property value. In their book *Freakonomics*, authors Levitt and Dubner reinforce this point, "real estate agents still get a higher price for their own homes than comparable homes owned by their clients." The complete study on this topic from the University of Chicago states, "properties owned by real estate agents sell for about 3.7 percent more than other properties."

Need more proof? What if I told you that there are case studies of properties that other brokerage couldn't sell. The deals expired, and were then listed by Sperry Van Ness. Guess what happened - same property, same market – different strategy, different results.

Case Study #1

Property Type	Broker	List Price	Days on Market	Number of Offers	Highest Offer Made	Status
Apartment Building	National Firm	$4,650,000	180	1	$4,100,000	Didn't Sell
Same property, re-listed by Sperry Van Ness	Sperry Van Ness	$4,650,000	90	5	$4,500,000	$4,500,000

Case Study #2

Property Type	Broker	List Price	Days on Market	Number of Offers	Highest Offer Made	Status
Apartment Building	Regional Broker	$7,000,000	90	2	$5,500,000	Didn't Sell
Same property, re-listed by Sperry Van Ness	Sperry Van Ness	$7,100,000	60	5	$7,200,000	$7,200,000

Case Study #3

Property Type	Broker	List Price	Days on Market	Number of Offers	Highest Offer Made	Status
Commercial Land	National Broker	$1,400,000	180	3	$1,300,00	Didn't Sell
Same property, re-listed by Sperry Van Ness	Sperry Van Ness	Listed with no price given	21	7	$1,475,000	$1,475,000

Case Study #4

Property Type	Broker	List Price	Days on Market	Number of Offers	Highest Offer Made	Status
Retail Center	Regional Broker	$12,500,000	270	10	$12,100,000	Didn't Sell
Same property, re-listed by Sperry Van Ness	Sperry Van Ness	$12,500,000	21	5	$12,500,000	$12,500,000

This realization came twenty years ago: marketing to the entire brokerage community and sharing one's commission 50/50 with other brokers – even one's own competition, is the only way to work in the client's best interest. This is what brought the once small Southern California based two-broker firm to status as one of the nation's fastest growing firms with 800 brokers in more than 100 markets nationwide. And as they continue this rapid period of growth, more clients are getting significantly higher returns when selling their properties – and that's a value that can't be disputed.

Now that you know the dirty little secret of commercial real estate, maybe you're ready to handle the politics and sausage thing. Sometimes the truth isn't pretty—but it's still good to know.

Red Flags when Selling Your Property

If your broker makes any one of these statements, consider it a red flag.

1. We don't have to list your property; I already have a buyer for you.

2. I have a pretty good idea of who the typical buyer is going to be for this property. We can save a lot of time by not marketing it and just completing the transaction.

3. I don't work with outside brokers.

4. If I do work with outside brokers, they will have to get their commission from their client—I won't share it with them.

5. If I do work with outside brokers, I will give them some of my commission, but half of it because I incur more cost as the listing agent.

6. I know your property has only been on the market for two days, but I already found a buyer.

7. In most cases, I represent both the buyer and the seller.

8. I know so many buyers, that we don't have to use other sources.

9. I'm going to try to sell the property on my own for sixty days, then I'll market it.

10. Who needs an outside broker— I've got five buyers for every property I list.

Brandstorming Questions

1. Are there inherent weaknesses in my industry's business model?

2. How can we change a model to put our company in a different category from the competition?

3. Is cooperating with the competition - and even paying them - an option for my company?

Strategy # 9:

Get in on the ground floor of a trend

Quagga - *www.quagga.com*

Peter Drucker once said, "People who take risks generally make about two big mistakes a year. People who don't take risks generally make about two big mistakes a year."

Quagga co-founder and President Scott Knorp is taking risks – but so far, he's not making mistakes, he's making history. By getting in on the ground floor of VoIP (Voice over Internet Protocol) nearly four years ago, he is forging ahead in new territory and leaving potential competitors on the periphery of the technological landscape.

"VoIP is the fastest growing segment of the telecom industry. Even the most conservative estimates predict revenue of $45 billion by 2007," according to Quagga co-founder and general managing partner Ken Apperson. VoIP enables you to make telephone calls with a broadband Internet connection instead of traditional analog phone line. You can call people who also have a VoIP system or in some cases, anyone with a phone number – local, long distance, mobile and international numbers. You can even call multiple people simultaneously at no extra charge.

"Quagga is aligned with the elite manufacturers in this space and understands the technology better than anyone - and the technology is complex," says Apperson. He and Knorp are industry veterans who teamed with other industry veterans to form the company. Knorp admits, "Even I didn't realize exactly how complex it was when I started the business three and a half years ago."

So imagine how intimidating that complexity can be to the technologically challenged business owner who might benefit from these services. Quagga has been able to remove the anxiety factor with a brand that incorporates humor, leveraged throughout the company. The Quagga website flashes classic song lyrics that incorporate high tech text such as:

"You ain't nothin' but an analog."
"I'll get by with a little help from my tech."
and everyone's favorite,
"Good, good, good - good VoIPrations."

A photo of happy people "doing the Quagga" helps web visitors feel at home in a strange new world. Even the company name evokes smiles. It was inspired by the African Quagga, an animal which is half zebra and half horse. "Although it's been extinct since the late 19th century," says Knorp, "we felt the animal was a perfect symbol of convergence." The name has also proven to be a good ice breaker for their salespeople who find that during their cold calls, prospects are more likely to giggle than hang up.

"Our industry is so complex, we like to make our message more folksy and accessible; it's also who we are – its part of our culture." So is their method of selling – which encompasses the breadth of a one-stop shop and the depth of industry experts in each category. "Ken comes from the phone system world and I come from the peripheral world – headsets, conferencing. Our competitors focus on one or the other spaces, but we've been able to bring it all under one roof. Customers get one-stop shopping plus the advantage of having Quagga staff with a depth of expertise in each product type.

Another part of the brand promise is a more cooperative sales environment. "We have a teaming focus within the organization," says Knorp. Sales people bring each other in on sales meetings to expand product offerings and work out arrangements with each other on their commissions. While this is disconcerting for some neophytes, it is understood that this is part of the culture and is the best thing to do for the clients.

"We've worked hard to cultivate a fun culture and it's infectious to the customers," says Knorp. "They want to keep coming back. It's also attracted a lot of industry veterans to our workforce who are tired of the same old grind. That's why we've branded our self 'the new face of communication.'" Knorp believes if you develop the culture, everything else follows. And followers include customers like Boston Market, Cigna Healthcare and eBay. "Even before we had the company, we had buzz," he says.

The buzz enabled them to become a direct distributor for headsets which is not easy to do for a new company. "Once that happened we were able to bring in more credibility."

The companies currently using VoIP are the early adopters. "VoIP is the new paradigm for communication," according to Knorp. If you haven't heard of it yet, you'll see a lot more usage of it in the next five years. So as an early entrant into an emerging market, Quagga is well positioned to meet the needs of the later adapters and bring them into the Quagga tribe.

What about imitators? "There aren't a lot of imitators yet – we're still off a lot of people's radars – they don't quite understand what we're doing. Some are starting off in to the headset space and are trying to get into the VoIP," says Knorp. By getting in early on the technology with experienced professionals, Knorp has a first mover advantage over competitors who are still trying to figure out the complexities of the industry. The knowledge base of Knorp and his team creates inherent barriers to entry for newcomers. While the early adapters represent most of his current clients, he is positioned well for the next five years, when he anticipates higher receptivity by businesses who are ready to make words like VoIP and Quagga part of their new vernacular.

Brandstorming Questions

1. What are three emerging trends in my industry that my company may be able to exploit?

2. Can my company afford to get in on the ground floor of one of these trends and be a leader?

3. How can I leverage my status as a first mover in this trend?

4. If my company has a product that is difficult for clients to understand, what can I do to reduce the intimidation factor by using humor? Conversational copy on my materials? A more approachable image through my website?

Strategy # 10:

Up the *Wow!* Factor

High Point University - *www.highpoint.edu*

When was the last time you had a business meeting with your company's Director of *Wow?* Does that seem like an unusual event? For Nido Qubein, it's just another day at the office.

When Qubein became High Point University's President, just eighteen months prior to this writing, he brought with him a wealth of experience and a contagious exuberance that would forever change the school's brand promise and experience. Qubein is chairman of several companies including Great Harvest Bread Company (218 stores in 40 states) and Business Life (magazine publishing). He chairs the Executive Committee and serves on the Board of BB&T, the ninth largest financial institution in the U.S., with more than $120 billion in assets, and is on the board of La-Z-Boy, one of the largest retailers in the country with over $2 billion in sales.

Qubein also has years of experience in sales and keynote speaking and has written more than a dozen books. And those credentials bode well for the man that set out to identify a solid point of differentiation for his university – one of more than 3000 accredited U.S. universities, all competing for student enrollment.

Qubein explains, "We wanted to differentiate ourselves in a purposeful and substantive manner. We wanted to provide our students with an extraordinary education in a fun environment with caring people." With that mission in mind, he began to walk around campus, engaging in dialogues with students and observing the campus and its activities.

"I began to recognize that there were lots of little things that could evoke a sigh of '*unwow*.'" What's an *unwow*? According to Qubein, "It's a wall that needs painting; a worn doormat; a leaky roof; an employee that refers a student to another office saying 'we don't handle that here'; or a poorly written letter from the university that contains too many 'I's' and not enough 'you's.'" And so the Director of *Wow* position was created. The job is divided into two primary areas of responsibility. One is to get rid of the *unwows*. The other is to create *wow* experiences.

The *unwows* were removed first. As Qubein puts it, "One thousand *wows* can be wiped out with one *unwow*." And then, the *wows* were added. As you'll see, they're enough to make you want to enroll.

Imagine for a moment that you have been accepted as a student to High Point. You open your mailbox to find your acceptance letter – which is not a letter at all – it's a *diploma* of acceptance – you've just experienced your first *wow*, and a realization that something special lies ahead. You and your family attend freshmen orientation and are greeted by a friendly staff member bearing a basket of goodies. While attending High Point, you notice one evening that live bands are playing outside of each residence hall to greet students as they arrive. Every afternoon, a High Point branded ice cream truck jingles throughout the campus bearing complimentary frozen treats. Classical music is played on the promenade from 7:00 a.m. to 9:00 p.m. And then, there's the library. The library is equipped with plasma TVs playing educational channels that you can listen to with earphones. Watch the History Channel as you curl up with a blanket on a comfy sofa. Getting hungry? Enjoy a complimentary sandwich and beverage– as long as you're quiet. Or leave the library to read your book in the park by a waterfall. If you're out late, don't worry. After-dark valet parking will ensure a safe return to your campus residence. The next day, you attend a class about real world business experience taught by Qubein himself. Going home for summer vacation? Expect to receive a letter from High Point telling you how much you're missed.

The *wow* factor is not a new concept to Qubein. As chairman of the Great Harvest Bread Company (*www.greatharvest.com*), he ensures that music is played in their 200 plus stores throughout the country while the smell of fresh baked bread fills the air. What about samples? "We don't give samples," he says. "We give *amples*!" Amples are big hunks of bread with a slathering of honey or butter for hungry customers to devour. And what the company doesn't sell, they give to charity – a *wow* for the community.

Whether in a school or a bakery, *wow* experiences make people feel vested and keep them coming back for more. Qubein's creative approach originates from zero based thinking – if money was not a concern, what would you create? Of course, for most businesses, money is a concern – but it shouldn't stop any business leader from creating their own *wow* experiences. Qubein says, "*Wow* is not always about cost, it's about innovation – it's a mindset, a culture, and a natural extension of your being. It's an integrated strategy - not just single events."

So, does *wow* translate into results? Within eighteen months, Qubein raised $65 million without a campaign, a staff, a feasibility study or a brochure. He simply talked to people about his vision and strategy. At the time of this writing, the campus is undergoing a $100 million transformation including ten buildings under construction and thirteen under renovation. Freshman enrollment is up 31 percent. Inquiries for next year are up 64 percent. Student retention has increased from 82 to 93 percent. Impressed? Go ahead. Say it with me. *Wow.*

Qubein's Four Step Business Strategy

1. Have a clear vision you can explain in one sentence.

2. Know where you are, where you're going and how you're going to get there.

3. Employ practical systems - pie in the sky doesn't cut it.

4. Have consistent execution. Brand is a promise based on trust. Trust is the result of proven execution and delivery. Trust has to be experienced.

Five Values of Great Harvest Bread Company

1. Be loose and have fun.

2. Bake phenomenal bread.

3. Run fast to help customers.

4. Create strong, exciting bakeries.

5. Give generously to others.

Brandstorming Questions

1. What are my company's top five *unwows*? How can I omit them from the company?

2. What are *unwows* that, if removed, would have the biggest impact on the perception of my brand – remember these do not have to cost a lot of money –they just have to have impact.

3. Which *wows* could be added to have the same powerful impact?

4. How committed am I to removing *unwows* and creating *wows*? Am I willing to have a person oversee this element of the organization?

5. If I am in a situation where I can let people sample my product or service, how can I change samples to *amples*? In what situations can I up the ante and give something more than expected?

Strategy # 11:

Be the first in your category (then prepare to deal with imitators)

Essential Learning - *www.essentiallearning.com*

Pop quiz – how do you provide 4600 hours of training to 500 employees in sixty days?   Answer – call Essential Learning.

Essential Learning is the largest provider of e-learning programs to behavioral health and human services organizations, such as those that provide care for the mentally ill, developmentally disabled, or those with addictions.

Founders Sue Erskine, CEO, and President Lorraine Watson, Ph.D, a clinical psychologist, identified a need in the market that was not being met. "The large, for-profit corporations had e-learning programs in place, but nothing was available for the non-profit behavioral healthcare organizations," according to Erskine. "And these groups have strictly regulated requirements for employee training and continuing education."

Even though e-learning programs were available for nurses and other healthcare professionals on an individual, pay-as-you-go basis, nothing existed for the healthcare companies that employed them. Yet it is the company's responsibility to provide proof of training for their employees. In order to comply, each healthcare organization had to gather paperwork from various employees and track those who had and had not been trained - this was usually done manually. But when you combine stringent industry regulations, a variety of training requirements, and manual tracking systems, you run the risk of non-compliance, inaccurate information, and wide variances in training program content. One client describes her company's training program prior to working with Essential Learning as, "costly, time consuming, sporadic, disorganized, and inconsistently recorded."

Essential Learning had the cure. Erskine says, "We customized a learning management system like those used by large for-profit companies, but tailored it toward smaller non-profits." The system enables employees to take classes in their free time at home on their own computers. Essential Learning provides the healthcare organization with a library of more than 250 required coursework programs. The employer can track the progress of the program, through an automated reporting system and quickly determine which employees are in compliance and which need additional training.

The company has been in operation since June of 2002 and is already servicing 55,000 employees from 181 organizations in thirty-five states. As expected, when a company has a valuable and rare product, imitators will start to emerge. But Erskine maintains differentiation with additional services, offering one new course per month in addition to the 250+ that come with the system. She will even create six additional customized courses tailored to specific needs of the customer. Additionally, Essential Learning has just been designated as the exclusive e-learning partner for the National Council for Community Behavioral Healthcare, a non-profit association of 1,300 behavioral healthcare organizations that provide treatment and rehabilitation for mental illnesses and addiction disorders to nearly six million people in communities across the country. This is a huge boost to Essential Learning's credibility in the industry and another powerful differentiator. "They help us market Essential Learning to their members," according to Erskine. "It's a seal of approval for us."

With only twelve full time employees, Essential Learning has proven that a small company with a powerful brand can have a profound impact on an industry. There will be more imitators in the future, but Essential Learning's first mover advantage and their readiness to respond to competitive copycats will enhance their longevity. And their success means good news for the health and well being of our communities.

Brandstorming Questions

1. How can I help customers solve problems on their own by accessing our system?

   a. Pay for service – is there a web component that can help my clients increase efficiencies in their business? How would I structure this cost?

   b. Free Service - If I wouldn't charge for this service, how can I use the free service to improve the value of my brand, the perception of my company and lead to new sales opportunities?

   c. How would this service create a competitive advantage for me in my market?

Strategy # 12:

Make a connection

Wahoo's Fish Taco- *www.wahoos.com*

Wing Lam, co-founder of Wahoo's Fish Taco knows that making great food is only half of the branding equation - the other half is making great connections.

"Most sports themed restaurants tend to have memorabilia that kids today are out of touch with," says Lam. "They have black and white sports photos of people that are old or no longer with us. There's no bonding. Or, they'll show people in the major leagues that kids can't touch. There's a big disconnect."

Lam has spent his career making successful connections between his customers and local athletes since he opened his first Southern California restaurant in 1988 with brothers Ed and Mingo. Partner Steve Karfaridis joined the trio in 1990. Lam recalls, "When I started I had limited financial assistance from my parents. I found local heroes."

A surfer since his early days, Lam embraced the California culture by endorsing Southern California surfers, and later other local athletes. Patrons quickly responded to the theme which included surf memorabilia that covered almost every inch of wall space in the funky, casual eatery. Wahoo's also featured surf and sports videos and it was not unusual for guests to see the same surfer riding a wave on the monitor sitting next to them eating lunch. Some athletes would come in with their sponsored team one day and their families the next. Kids were thrilled to be eating in the same restaurant alongside their heroes.

Wahoo's became more than a restaurant. It represented a lifestyle and a local pride that resonated with customers. Some started to come in daily where staff would greet them by name. The connection was made and Lam continued his local endorsements.

"I always sponsored high school sports," he says. And several of the athletes have made it to the pro level. Lam invested in them early. Now, they're endorsing Wahoo's. "They want to give back," he says.

And what athlete wouldn't enjoy the hearty menu selections, each revealing Lam's own cultural diversity. The son of Chinese restaurateurs, he grew up in Brazil and Southern California, with frequent trips to Mexico and Hawaii. While in Mexico, he developed a taste for the fish tacos – a Wahoo is a fish from the mackerel family. After a day of sunshine and waves, hungry surfers wanted to eat something fresh, healthy and inexpensive, and the fish taco was often their food of choice. Lam imported the fish to Southern California, where residents proved to be a receptive audience. Other menu items include grilled Polynesian shrimp with soy sauce, Cajun seasoning, jack cheese, shredded green cabbage and fresh salsa. Or the Baja rolls made of spinach, cream cheese, chicken and salsa wrapped in a soft flour tortilla.

While he doesn't consider it health food, Lam says that local trainers often recommend the "clean" (relatively unprocessed) cuisine to their clients. The food is also featured at numerous local sporting events, sponsored by Lam. "You have to walk the talk," he says. "I support events in the mountains, beaches or skateboard parks. A good majority of people in Southern California have at one time either tried to participate or have participated in these sports, so a ten, twenty or thirty-year-old can relate to these events."

With athletes, fans, and good food at each event, it was only natural that musicians would follow. Lam recalls, "Some of the bands hired for the events began to hang out with the athletes. Soon, more bands started to become associated with us. One or two of them ended up hitting the charts, like the band blink-182. The pop-punk band from suburban San Diego has since achieved worldwide acclaim, and drummer Travis Barker is now a Wahoo's franchisee with two Southern California locations of his own. "We initially started franchising with people that we knew," says Lam. Today, there are forty-three Wahoo's in California, Colorado, Hawaii and Texas.

But keeping brand consistency can be a huge challenge when franchises start popping up in multiple locations. While Lam requires that the menu be kept intact, he lets each franchisee impart its own unique spin on the restaurant based on the area's local sports - after all, there aren't a lot of surfers in Colorado. In Austin, wakeboarding is popular; in other areas, the sport of choice might be jet skiing, mountain climbing, skateboarding or football. And as each theme is played out, more connections are made.

Lam is determined to keep his brand immersed in the culture, by focusing on his clients, not himself. He depicts this concept by comparing a football player who does a touchdown end zone dance, to a champion surfer who, after a triumphant win, avoids the showy self-celebratory antics. "When you're a free rider, there is no celebration. We're part of the culture. If you're going to be in the youth business, it's about being inclusive not being the 'look at me' guy."

The inclusion factor is also evident in his advertising which conveys a humorous and fun image rather than a direct sales approach. Headlines like "If it can satisfy whales, it can satisfy you" and "You never see fat mermaids, do you?" depict Lam's ability to have fun instead of going for the hard sell. "People don't want to be sold to; they want to discover things on their own" he says.

And the discovery will continue as Lam finds new ways to reach out to customers. He has recently partnered with Sector 9 Skateboards, an industry leader known for its high quality long board products. "As a skateboard company, they're already doing events." Lam's partnership will enable him to have a presence at the shows where he can do what he does best – make great food and great connections.

Brandstorming Questions

1. Do my clients have a connection when using my company's products or services?

2. Does that connection cause an emotional attachment?

3. What emotional components exist in my brand? Fear of losing money? Fear of looking older? Fear of failing health? Love of a particular lifestyle? Need to be glamorous? Need to connect with celebrities or heroes?

4. What can I do to improve the connection with my clients and my brand, my employees, my sales staff? What connections can be made by marketing the brand? During the use of the brand? After the product has been purchased?

Strategy # 13:

Help your prospects see you in a whole new light

Heart Gallery - *www.adoptuskids.com*

Diane Granito specializes in priceless works of art - priceless not because of the artist, but because of the subject matter. Each frame contains a photograph of a child in search of a family.

The Heart Gallery matches foster children with parents in a way that has never been done before. Professional photographers volunteer their services and create gallery quality photographs which capture the spirit of each child in every frame. The finished artwork is displayed in local art galleries or other high-traffic venues to be viewed by prospective adoptive parents. The positioning of these children in a favorable light has dramatically changed the perspective of the adoptive parents' views of children deemed "hard to place," a category which includes older children, minorities, and those in sibling groups.

At any given time, nearly 130,000 children in the U.S. foster care system are waiting to be placed with adoptive parents; 19,000 of them each year will "age out" of the system, turning eighteen without ever finding a family.

Granito founded the Heart Gallery in 2001. Already employed full time as an adoptive parent recruiter for the Protective Services Division of the New Mexico Children, Youth & Families Department, she was not looking for a new project. But one day an adoptive mother commented on the dismal mug shots of the foster children, often taken against a blank wall. She suggested that professionally taken photographs might be more compelling. Diane moved quickly on the idea. She didn't have a budget, but she did have a vision.

"I went to the Gerald Peters Gallery, a prestigious gallery in Santa Fe, thinking they would never say yes," Granito recalls. "Their response was overwhelming." The first project quickly came into focus with fifty of the area's finest photographers. Twelve hundred people attended the first opening and were serenaded by country singer Randy Travis. "We got media attention from the very beginning, pitching to the Associated Press, and *CameraArts* Magazine. We placed six children the first night alone – older children with special needs."

The media frenzy flourished, creating results that Granito could have never imagined. "There are now Heart Galleries in more than forty states and in foreign countries," she adds. And their placement results are astonishing. Granito states that on average, only about 5 percent of prospective parents actually end up adopting a child. The Heart Galleries in Florida, New Mexico, and Maine currently have adoption completion rates of 41 percent, 50 percent, and 58 percent respectively.

Granito and the other Heart Gallery planners around the country have been smart about placing these photographs where they can make the biggest impact, by both promoting the brand and capturing the essence of each hosting city. Los Angeles held an opening at the Kodak Theatre, giving the children an opportunity to walk the red carpet. A national opening in Washington DC, sponsored by the Federal Children's Bureau, featured fifty photographs on Capitol Hill where the Senators enter the building and another fifty at Union Station. Eighty thousand people passed by the Union Station portraits each day, giving high visibility to the portraits. This major brand outreach took the message directly to legislators so that they might ask themselves, "what's going on with legislation in my state?'"

The spectacular media events were not part of Granito's original job description, but she states that the opportunity was "too good to pass up." She compares the Heart Gallery concept to online dating services like *Match.com.*

"If you were looking for a life mate online, you wouldn't use your driver's license photo or list your negative attributes." So why shouldn't the children have the same opportunity to put their best face and story forward?

"We're now working on 'Write for Kids,' which will go hand in hand with the Heart Gallery" Says Granito.   Volunteer writers will add stories of each child to create an even stronger emotional impact to the already compelling photos. She explains, "Instead of the usual, 'Johnny's in fifth grade and struggles in school,' the story might read, 'Johnny walked into the garage on Father's Day and gave his foster father a card and a big hug.' Why focus on negative traits - don't we all struggle at times?"

She recalls the struggle of one photographer who simply could not get two young brothers – Elijah and Isaiah - to smile. When the photographer called in tears, Granito assured her that it was all right if the children didn't smile. The photographer had captured the feelings and emotions that she saw through the camera's lens. Granito says, "The final photograph stopped one family in their tracks. They said, 'these boys need us.'" They adopted Elijah and Isaiah just in time – the boys were about to be placed in an institution. Granito says, "Now they're the best behaved kids, are no longer on medications and are at a grade level or above in school. It just shows you what unconditional love can do."

Before photo: Elijah and Isaiah wouldn't smile

After photo: the boys with their new adoptive parents

Another child, Faye, was adopted by the very photographer who took her Heart Gallery photo. "Faye was ten years old and a handful," says Granito. But Faye's new adoptive Mom and Dad gave her time and love. Granito says, "Today, Faye is just an amazing girl. She's a classical violinist and a student at the Waldorf School, where she excels in art. She is blossoming. It's like these families grab the kids before they're going off the edge and say, 'We're here for you.' Once the kids truly believe that someone won't give up on them, the turnaround is amazing."

Diane's clever leveraging of the media has helped to shape this brand in the minds of the consumers while diminishing the stigma of child protective services agencies. "Everywhere we took the program, there were positive articles. Often you're fighting the image of a protective services agency – not just creating an image of the Heart Gallery. Protective service organizations do good work under challenging conditions. Most people don't know that, in New Mexico and many other states, there has been a 25 percent or higher increase of children taken into the system each year due to the methamphetamine (meth) crisis. Fewer of them are able to go back to their families, who just can't get off the meth. In New Mexico and other states, we also have to work with multimillion dollar budget cuts. That hurts our ability to do out-reach that was done in the past, like run television, radio and print ads, as we simply don't have the funds."

But Granito has used the media to make her case. ABC News named the Heart Gallery photographers "Person of the Week" and 20/20 ran two segments on the project. Others including *CBS Sunday Morning*, CNN, MSNBC, Nickelodeon, *People, Parade, USA Weekend* and scores of other newspapers and magazines are keeping the positive buzz going. "That's how the branding took place and will continue," she says.

One of Granito's next moves will be to help promote the purchase of display board systems to be placed in airports and major malls, showing the photos and stories of the children. "We'll switch out the pictures as children are adopted. When people go to the mall and see these faces looking out at them, it will stay with them. Adoption is a big step – this might open their minds."

Granito adds, "Each board will also display information on how to adopt a child along with before and after photos. It will help us to dispel myths about adoption – it's not $10,000 to adopt a child – it's free – you even get a subsidy from the state. In many states, you can adopt if you are gay or lesbian. We don't want people to eliminate themselves based on myths."

Granito's branding efforts have been as good as those of any marketing professional. Her passion and focus have reframed a stigmatized industry in the mind of the consumer by creating a new image of love, strength and hope.

Brandstorming Questions

1. How can I showcase my product in a completely different light ?

   a. If I have a tangible product that might include photographing the product in a non-traditional setting. For example, a retail store that sells clothing and hardware might show a woman in an elegant dress, holding a power drill. The photo catches the people's attention and enforces the fact that the store offers a variety of products.

   b. If I have an intangible product, it might be by classifying the product in a category that is not obvious –for example – if I am a dentist that specializes in painless techniques, I may promote the atmosphere of my office which is more like a spa, with relaxing music, exotic teas, and a waterfall in the waiting area, to reinforce the relaxing atmosphere.

Strategy # 14:

Shake up your vertical market

Vampire Wine - *www.vampire.com*

Michael Machat is taking a healthy bite out of the wine industry's market share.

With a flair for business and for the dramatic, he founded Vampire Wine. An entertainment attorney by day, Machat can't confirm or deny the presence of vampires on his payroll, but every detail of his brand is so eerily consistent, it just might keep you guessing.

For one thing, the winery is based in Transylvania, Romania and run by an English philosopher and his Romanian wife – an almost too good to be true brand scenario. That's because Machat came up with the brand first, and the product second.

"I always thought it would be great if someone came up with a product called Vampire Wine and that the vineyards would be in Transylvania," he recalls. At the time he had no idea that Romania was the tenth largest wine producing country in the world.

When Machat decided to bring the wine to the U.S., he first approached Pepsi, then the distributors of Stolichnaya Vodka and the only U.S. importer of Romanian Wine. "They thought I was crazy and turned me down, but they did give me the names of some contacts in Romania." As it turns out, the Romanian contacts were as disinterested as Pepsi when he approached them.

"They had just gotten through 45 years of communism and just didn't get marketing as a concept in general – let alone the marketing of vampires."

But when have you known an attorney to give up without a fight? He persisted in finding a way to market the product in the U.S., counting on the fact that existing wineries were missing an important demographic group –Gen X'rs who find traditional wine somewhat stuffy or intimidating.

Like the movie *Sideways* which caused an 18 percent surge of supermarket Pinot Noir sales, Machat is doing his part to bring wine into the main stream. He sold his first bottle to Alice Cooper and MCA records in London in 1988. In 1989, he sold 672 bottles to the Anne Rice Fan club in New Orleans and received an onslaught of letters of appreciation primarily from young fans.

This confirmed his theory about the need for a wine product to a younger audience, but it wasn't easy getting the product to his newly identified market.

"Getting wine distributors to accept the product's credibility was a challenge," says Machat. "We started in New York City, believing it would be the most receptive market." Machat's media savvy generated publicity from *Elle* magazine, *USA Today*, *The New York Times*, and MTV, all prompting curious drinkers to ask for the wine by name at their local retailers. And the demand for Vampire wine began.

"We started out with red wines - Merlot and Cab - then added Pinot Noir and Pinot Grigio. At $6 to $10 per bottle, Vampire's Pinot is comparable to those from Italy, priced at $15 and above." Today Vampire wine is the top selling Eastern European wine in the U.S.

But the quality of the wine is just one part of the equation. Machat's attention to every branding detail is uncanny. His primarily red and black website (*www.vampire.com*) has an exciting entertainment vibe, letting viewers know that this is not their father's winery. Packaging is displayed with the company's signature blood dripping "V" logo. Site visitors can join the Vampire Wine Club to receive regular wine shipments accompanied by a different vampire video. Music downloads, vampire wallpaper and even the site's trident- like cursor, add to the brand experience. The site's written messaging is as striking as its rich visual imagery:

> Now, Transylvania's most cherished secret, the blood of the vine, has once again been released. Made by a master winemaker, in accordance with ancient secrets of folklore, combined with modern vinification techniques, Vampire Wines continue to ignite the nocturnal passions.

"Most wine companies take themselves too seriously" says Machat. "They create a product that is misunderstood and intimidating." Machat believes that people drink wine for one primary reason - to change their state of consciousness. "It's a question of entertainment and I think the wine trade misses that – it's kind of like getting into the technicalities of how a toaster works rather than just giving someone a piece of toast. Taste and flavor are merely the third factor that comes to mind when someone decides to buy wine."

He further categorizes wine makers as "Chino and dress shirt wearing types" that cater to markets of the same ilk, and abandon everyone else to the beer companies. "We are the wine of choice for the new wine drinkers," says Machat, "friendly, entertaining and approachable."

He does have some advice for his competitors. "Fire your marketing departments and hire people from the record industry. Managing a brand is like managing a band. It's about creating excitement and selling the experience." When Machat extended his product line to include Vodka, he had a pleasant surprise. Vampire Vodka was created with a deep red color and viscosity to look like blood. "We didn't know it would turn your lips red," states Machat, but drinkers love their crimson grins, which only add to brand experience and buzz.

Other products include a cherry flavored energy drink called **VAMP N.R.G.** And don't forget the kids –Machat also makes Dracola - the world's first red cola for children of the night.

His foresight has given him a jump start in an industry that is just discovering the very market that he's been serving for years. According to *Forbes* Magazine, vintners Bennett Lane of California and Ravenswood Winery are now sponsoring NASCAR teams. Nappa's Don Sebastiani and Sons are positioning their wines with irreverent and easy to pronounce names like Screw Kappa Nappa and Smoking Loon. A wine from Click Wine Group called Fat Bastard invites drinkers to submit their party photos to its website. Other mainstream wineries are using younger spokespeople, colorful labels, pint size bottles, and even metallic pink cans, focusing on the fashion and image of a new generation. And the younger crowd is lapping it up. U.S. wine sales in food and drugs stores and wine outlets are up 10 percent over last year, hitting the $4.5 billion mark. This includes Costco, the largest wine retailer in the nation with sales that reached $700 million, an 8 percent increase over the previous year.

Sometimes it takes an outsider to shake up an industry. While the competition is heating up, Machat continues to gain loyal fans. He is now the go-to person for all vampire promotional products and services, including the sponsorship of movie premiers like *Underworld Evolution* starring Kate Beckinsale and Scott Speedman of TV's late 90's Felicity fame. Machat even plans to create the "Inn at the Vampire Vineyards" complete with late night, lantern led tours of the wine's Transylvanian home. Machat continues to create new and exciting methods to position his product in an industry that's ripe for change.

Brandstorming Questions

1. Is my vertical market due for a shakeup? What can I do that is unexpected? What would be unpredictable in this industry? (i.e., a creative way to tell my company's story)

2. How can I incorporate this concept to show that my product is truly different and unique?

Strategy # 15:

Make it practical

Jude Frances Jewelry - *www.judefrances.com*

Four years ago, photographer Jude Steele and interior designer Frances Gadbois, two striking Southern California based beauties, had $9,000 and a plan to launch a jewelry business. Having no background in the industry, they created their first product line consisting of seven pair of earrings, but couldn't get any buyers to return their phone calls. In just a few years, they have turned their business into a $10 million company - and now buyers are calling them.

Their growth is remarkable especially considering the fact that businesses owned by female entrepreneurs rarely reach $1 million in annual revenues. The Washington-based Center for Women's Business Research reports that while 48 percent of all privately held U.S. firms are owned by women, only 3 percent of them have achieved the seven-figure milestone of success.

So how did Gadbois and Steele beat the odds? It took more than just a quality product to compete for space beneath the glass case with well established designers. Their creative strategy prevailed over a limited budget and an industry with high barriers to entry. Gadbois says, "I've always said that it's easy to be creative when you have no money." And since money was not an option for the team, creativity prevailed.

"We started out by just banging on doors and having our friends wear our jewelry," says Gadbois. "Once we started getting lists of key stores, Jude would spend hours every day cold calling them and they always had a million reasons why they couldn't talk to her." The women sent products to the store which were sent back. They knew they had to find a way to make their gems sparkle in the minds of their prospects.

Inspired by the green apples Gadbois used to decorate her home, they began to photograph their line of diamonds, pink tourmaline, garnets and citrine using the fruit as a backdrop. Gadbois says, "We photographed on the apple, and it became our color scheme." The women placed their nature inspired photos in boxes along with gourmet toffee, using bright green and black packaging. They sent the gift boxes to their prospects and suddenly, their calls were being returned. The two entrepreneurs knew they were on to something.

A friend with connections in the industry helped them get into their first jewelry trade show in Las Vegas, which is a coup in and of itself, since most vendors have to get on long waiting lists to participate. Steele recalls, "Our booth was back by the bathroom. We didn't have money to decorate it so we used black velvet and green apples. No one had heard of us, but so many stores came by because they got the gifts." Their next show in New York was preceded by gift boxes to prospects with green jelly beans and a taxi cab along with the green apple photos. "Most of our competitors sent cards with photos of their jewelry on white backgrounds," says Steele. "We sent our gifts via FedEx. They spent their entire budget on photography – we spent ours on packaging." The team soon saw their green apples turn to gold, receiving a Golden Apple Award for two consecutive years for their trade show exhibit.

Clarity and care make diamonds – and brands – sparkle.

The trade shows paid off. Niemen Marcus was the first store to accept their product line. Gadbois says, "That gave us instant credibility. It was a great calling card." Others stores followed. The women's product line is now in 29 Niemen Marcus stores, 4 Bloomingdales, more than 80 independent stores, and online with Niemen Marcus, Bergdorf Goodman and Bloomingdales – all done without advertising, no business loans and minimal debt. Gadbois says, "We don't do things unless we can afford to."

Once they got the attention of their prospects, they were able to give them a product that was truly different. The gems are both beautiful and practical – a contradiction in an industry which tends to focus on fashion over feasibility. Jude Frances jewelry has interchangeable charms that attach to hoop earrings, posts or necklaces. This gives the wearer the ability to buy a standard piece and build on it for a variety of looks. The affordable prices points, ranging from $300 to $2,000, make these gems every girl's best friend. In fact, Steele and Gadbois refer to their products as "everyday chic," making them a perfect accessory for everything from jeans to eveningwear.

The line has now expanded to include necklaces, rings, bracelets and cuffs. They now have new product lines including a bridal collection, a silver collection and a men's line. Even though the pieces have been purchased by celebrities including Oprah, Steel and Gadbois remain focused on their core market – women who want quality and value.

Now that they have garnered well-earned industry recognition, the duo is ensuring that the brand is kept in high regard through exceptional customer service. They are both approachable and accessible. "We bend over backwards for our clients," says Gadbois. Ensuring a positive brand experience from initial contact throughout the sales cycle, they have built a business that continues to thrive. Steele and Gadbois have shown that newcomers and small business owners have an opportunity to do what the larger competitors can't, don't or won't do- provide good old fashioned service, thoughtful gifts, accessibility, and a personalized brand experience for both their clients and the end users. Because small businesses don't have big names to fall back on and having a quality product isn't a differentiator – it's a minimum requirement for entry. Steele and Gadbois have set themselves apart by making their jewelry very much like themselves - beautiful and practical.

Brandstorming Questions

1 Does my product or service have qualities that are practical, more accessible, and high quality at an affordable price? If not, is this a strategy worth pursuing?

2. If I do not have a lot of money to advertise, what creative methods can I use to showcase my product in terms of gifts to clients, trade shows or other creative methods to make my brand known?

Strategy # 16:

Be the best, not the biggest

DSN Software - *www.dsnsoftware.com*

"We compete with giants," says Charley Black, Founder of DSN Software. Giants with names like Eastman Kodak and Henry Schein, Inc, with $14.2 billion and $4.6 billion in sales respectively - giants which could have sent smaller entrepreneurs running, but not Black. In fact some of these giants are the greatest source of new customers for his company which is now the fastest growing dental practice management software company in the country. Black's strategy? Don't be the biggest. Be the best.

Bo Burlingame, author and editor-at-large for *Inc.* magazine, has branded companies that have chosen to be great instead of big as "small giants" in his book of the same name. He identifies several companies which "passed up the growth treadmill—and focused on greatness instead." These companies often focus on business goals such as offering better working environments, customer service, or community contributions.

In the case of DSN, greatness came from being at the heels of giants and getting a unique perspective on how not to run a business. Black was able to observe the sluggishness of corporate monoliths in response to customer needs and the vulnerability of rapidly growing companies cracking beneath the weight of mergers and acquisitions. After all, didn't business consultant and author Peter Drucker say that mergers and acquisitions are what companies do when they run out of creative ways of growing the business?

Black's creative thinking lead him to realize that rapid growth and deteriorating customer service were the competitors' Achilles' heels that he could parlay into a powerful brand differentiation strategy.

Black purchased the company, which initially offered both hardware and software, in 1989 from the dentist who originally owned it. At the time, he thought it would be a good retirement project for him, but I suspect that he's working harder now than ever.

"When I came here, there was no product standardization - virtually every product shipped was different," he recalls. "I engaged in a two-year mission to create a specialized product that works for all of our clients, with added customized features based on specific industry needs. For example, clients may specialize in general dentistry or oral surgery. One needs medical billing, the other doesn't. One is long term care, the other isn't." Black's product development resulted in greater operational efficiencies for the company while still giving the client a customized solution.

Black's next move was to narrow the scope of the offering to software only and expand from a regional to a national market. "We developed relationships with hardware people around the country. They are brand evangelists for us – we take good care of those people."

Giant sized competitors don't often provide the individual attention offered at DSN. In fact, Black refers to his company's product as service, not software. He's also cognizant that as his own business grows, he won't follow in his competitor's big footsteps. "It will be a challenge for us in the future. As you get to a place where you have so many clients, it's harder to deliver the personal service, but I'm trying to find ways, as we grow, to improve, rather than degrade our service."

Black's *CRM* (Customer Relationship Management) software enables his call center staff to see not only which client is calling, but the names of key people in the office, and even the weather at the client's location.

"My competitors are not using this type of system. But it's not just about the technology that enables you to speak with your clients– it's about who you hire to do the support. Our clients would rather talk to us than use their instruction manuals."

Black was also smart about hiring the right people to help promote the company, enlisting the help of Manhattan-based Dovecote Advertising (*www.dovecoteny.com*). Dovecote created an ad strategy by doing something that many companies forget to do – focus on the brand, not the product.

Doug Kim of Dovecote says, "One of the things we tried to do was to pinpoint a specific kind of doctor who would find DSN compelling. This is the doctor who doesn't mind a boutique software company. There are people who want big and that's fine. But DSN is for those people who appreciate a product that's engineered to the nth degree. We defined a very specific target audience and talk to them in an engaging intelligent manner."

The strategy is clear in Dovecote's advertising campaign for DSN which employed a more copy-heavy, empathetic approach, rather than the hard sell, features and benefits strategy of their competitors. Kim says, "We chose a more engaging, intelligent style to reflect a more intelligently engineered software."

Kim and partner Chris Eng used a clever conversational format to convey the personality of the brand. One ad shows a photo of Black fishing and a headline that reads, "There are two things we care about – one is fishing, the other is software." It's a compelling one liner that leads into a message about the business of practice management. A caption with a map of DSN's home base near Seattle states, "We're located in Western Washington, a region known for its fishing and software." This type of ad often scares business executives because it's not the traditional hard sell. But it hooks readers and begins the evolution of a brand personality.

Another ad headline reads, "Anal Retentiveness Available for Purchase" and is followed by a story about the pursuit of perfection. Dovecote has been able to personify a technology brand and in doing so, enabled the personality of the company to shine through.

The ads have garnered additional business for the company, and once on board, customers are likely to refer new business. Fifty percent of DSN's business comes from customer referrals. Black attributes this to the belief that people like to be treated by their suppliers in a manner that is similar to how they treat their own clients. He says, "Our clients are the higher end dental offices. They provide a high-touch Nordstrom type experience to their patients. And we provide our clients with the same service."

Photos can help consumers identify with a brand personality

The trend towards a preference for boutique firms and niche products is growing in other industries as well, despite the historical "bigger is better" mentality of the business world. Once viewed as benign low-volume players, some niche companies have now become significant competitive threats. Who would have thought that when the soft drink industry showed signs of going flat last year, sports drink companies were responsible? Even more surprising is that sports drinks are expected to out earn every soft drink category in the next three years. This should validate the small business owner, who knew all along that by keeping a boutique firm status, customers would respond. And Black is no exception.

It's a service that won't be sacrificed for growth. He explains, "When Kodak got involved with dental software the theory was that a company could buy smaller companies, group them together, and create one software solution that could support 10,000 people instead of 5,000. That might be a good accounting theory, but it's doesn't work for us."

But Black's own accounting doesn't seem to be suffering as a result. The company has been growing at 15 percent a year for the last four years. DSN's steady growth has given the company and brand a favorable prognosis.

Brandstorming Questions

1. Can my company be a small giant in my industry?

2. If my priority is not being the biggest, then what product or service will enable me to be the best?

3. How will I communicate that difference through my advertising, website, and sales force?

4. How can I leverage my difference to customers through a customer relationship management program?

Strategy # 17:

Give in to instant gratification

Impact Engine - *www.impactengine.com*

"Instant gratification has caught on fast in the marketplace," says Neil Greer, co-founder of Impact Engine. Business executives often don't have time to contact a graphic designer when creating a last minute promotional solution. And now they don't have to.

Impact Engine offers a web based tool at *www.impactengine.com* that enables individuals to create their own professional websites and flash presentations via an easy to use wizard format which incorporates graphics, photography, music, text and links. One product called Presentation Engine can be created in minutes, and makes even the most technologically challenged look like a graphics pro.

The product can be used as a website, a sales presentation tool, or an e-mail icon which enables the recipient to launch the presentation on their own. Changes can be made in real time to immediately update or alter the presentation – even after it's been sent to someone.

For example, if a real estate agent sends the presentation via email to an email list and the property price changes one month later, he can make the changes from his computer. Clients who have already received the presentation can click back on the link and receive the updated information. The product also keeps metrics on the number of presentations sent, number of times opened and the time it was opened, so the salesperson knows who viewed it and can follow up with a phone call.

Now everyone can have a customized, branded presentation to sell any product or service. And at $1700/year for unlimited use of the tool, clients can feel good about their economics as well as their aesthetics.

Greer, along with co-founders Bryan Depew and Bennett Blank started the company because of what Greer calls "the scalability of markets to adjust to an ever changing advertising landscape." He explains, "In the 60's and 70's a company's job was to create the one ad that everyone would respond to. Today, you may have to change your collateral daily to adjust. You need the right tools and strategies. It's not about the one message – it's about the thousand unique awesome messages."

"Marketers today are using every point of differentiation they can and are using social networking and highly reigned messages for niche markets," says Greer. "You may have one product that you sell to the Latino market, the Seattle market, and the Orange County, California market." With Impact Engine, you can make changes that will speak to each market's particular nuances.

"We sell into defense, tourism, professional sports, the media business, about and every major vertical." About 30 percent of their business comes from the real estate presentation product.

The company has been in business for six years and initially had to be careful about how to market the product cost effectively. They looked to Google which accounted for almost 90 percent of the company's growth. In one year, they tracked 600 percent growth using Google. Greer says, "I'm a firm believer in controlled cost case studies that can be extrapolated. I don't just blow money – I define the market and try to gauge what works. The bottom line is, Google users are 75 percent more likely to buy online products because they're down to the decision making time and ready to spend money. They go to the search engine and say, 'I can't believe I put this off.'" Since the Impact Engine product creates a fast, professional and cost-effective solution, their product was a perfect match for the search engine. And that's instant gratification at work.

"As the company evolves we're seeing that the Impact Engine strategy applied to different marketplaces. We also developed an advertising product that people can only buy through an advertising medium. Media companies buy the product to create instant impact flash advertisements in a fraction of the time. The media representative can present this to clients before the client even buys the ad. This helps the client envision the online ad in a way that can't be done on paper. Prior to Impact Engine, the production costs of flash advertisements were prohibitive. By making the system available to clients, media companies can create cost-effective advertising solutions to increase online advertising click through rates."

But the success is not without complexities. Greer says, "The blessing and the curse is that we differentiated the product so well, that we created a niche market. But like most niche marketing, when you try to push the bounds in one product line, you run into barriers. We addressed that by starting to create new packaged products with the same platform but for different industries. If you're a niche product company and you're thinking how to grow, don't make your niche product homogenous. Make other products that fit larger niches."

The media product yields $50,000 per year in revenue per client as compared to the lower cost individual use product. By expanding the product line to another market, Greer was able to create a significantly higher profit margin with the same technology without diluting the brand. Either way, Greer is satisfying and gratifying his customers every time.

Brandstorming Questions

1. If clients could have instant gratification in my industry, what would that look like?

2. How can I shorten the times my customer has to wait:

   a. To access my services in person?

   b. On the web?

   c. In receiving products through mail?

   d. In having conflicts resolved?

Simple Green - *www.simplegreen.com*

It wasn't easy being green in 1972. The term "environmentally friendly" was not a trend, a fad, or even a significant consideration to most people – certainly not those in the chemical cleaning industry. But Bruce FaBrizio's decision to create an environmentally friendly cleaning product was not prompted by trends or fad. It was prompted by conviction.

FaBrizio worked his way through Occidental College by delivering chemicals. One day at a worksite, he witnessed a horrible accident caused by the very chemicals an employee was carrying. "I vowed that I would never let that happen again," he says. He talked to his father about developing a product that was safe for people and for the environment. That product was Simple Green. But the cleaning solution that has now reached unprecedented success almost never came into being, enduring a series of rejections and false accusations before reaching its current status as a near $100 million company with a presence in forty-two countries.

When Bruce and his father started the company, they couldn't find a single bank that was willing to finance a "green" idea proposed by two Italian Americans with no money and no formal business education. So FaBrizio went to the streets in search of less "traditional" financing. He eventually found a lender, of sorts - let's call him Rocco. Rocco was happy to fork over the green - at 50 percent interest of course. It was an offer FaBrizio couldn't refuse.

In the early days, FaBrizio had to be all things to the company. He recalls, "We manufactured on Saturday, sold on Monday, Wednesday and Friday, delivered on Tuesday and Thursday, and we rounded all sales figures to even numbers so I could keep the books on Sunday."

And the numbers needed to be good. FaBrizio had spent $3 million on research and development over a ten year period working with specialists from Duke University. It was an exorbitant amount of money that his own colleagues thought was excessive, but FaBrizio was unshaken in his resolve to create a product with three criteria: safety, effectiveness and simplicity of use.

But the selling of a green product was anything but simple. No one believed the product would work. The company was not yet making money. FaBrizio's accountants told him that things weren't going well. The debt was unbelievable; the cost of research unfathomable; the interest from Rocco unthinkable. One weekend FaBrizio couldn't make payroll. He took $8700 to Las Vegas and put it on a craps table, trying to turn it into $20,000. He recalls, "Thirty minutes later, we were broke. I had to fire myself – I went on commission only and I had to pay Rocco anyway." FaBrizio sold his house and car to pay his debt to Rocco. But there were other bills due.

He also owed 18 suppliers $165,000 and asked them to put a moratorium on their interest with a guarantee that he would pay them 50 percent on whatever he collected if they wouldn't put him out of business. Their signed agreements remain in FaBrizio's safe to this day – and they've all long since been paid in full. But the victory came at a great price. FaBrizio recalls, "The pressures led to my father's demise. He passed away in December of 1979."

FaBrizio grew even stronger in his convictions and continued with the company which he had to grow while still taking care of the increasing high interest debt he had incurred. After his father's death, the accountants continued to caution FaBrizio. The company wasn't doing well. They weren't going to make it. FaBrizio's mantra to them became, "everything's going to be all right."

FaBrizio got his first big break when he convinced JC Penny to give him a national contract to clean their service bays. The people at JC Penny started to realize the cleaner's potential for industrial as well as home use when they discovered their own mechanics were taking the product out of the 55 gallon storage drums and bringing it home in their Thermos's. JC Penny agreed to carry the product in their stores in 1985, but store operators mistakenly placed the product in the lawn and garden section. Anything called Simple Green must be a plant food, right?

As the business began to grow, competitors became nervous. FaBrizio recalls, "Clorox Corporation filed a suit against us in the state of California, stating that I was the Jim Jones of the environmental cleaning business." Clorox said that Simple Green's claims were false and filed suit on behalf of the Consumer Product Safety Commission. The case made its way to the Federal Trade Commission and the U.S. Attorney General. FaBrizio had to go to Washington DC to defend himself and his product against seven different legal organizations to prove his product safety – if he failed to do so, Simple Green would be shut down and the only thing FaBrizio would be cleaning were the floors of the jailhouse he would ultimately be sentenced to.

But how could a little guy with a lot of debt stand up against Clorox and the U.S. government? Simple. FaBrizio had something they weren't expecting. Remember the $3 million of voluntary research he conducted with Duke University before he launched the product – the costly research that everyone said was crazy? It was that very data that vindicated FaBrizio. It even got him a new client – the U.S. Government. Now that he had their attention he demonstrated the product to NASA. He showed its effectiveness by cleaning their aircrafts with Simple Green – and then did something that none of his competitors could do – he drank the product. While he does not recommend doing this (apparently a shot of the green packs a bit of a gastrointestinal punch), the U.S. Armed Forces now purchases 80 percent of their biodegradable cleaning products from Simple Green.

Today, Sunshine Maker's Inc., the parent company of Simple Green, has become purely a marketing management company with 85 people and double digit growth for thirty consecutive years. FaBrizio adds, "We have several new products using nano technology to clean and polish stainless steel and aluminum. After twenty years of failure, we cracked the code to safely clean the skin of airplanes." Extreme Simple Green has just hit the aerospace industry and is being well received.

Simple Green doesn't just target the big corporations. They have also achieved significant growth at trade shows targeting every type of buyer. Product differentiation has become obvious from the company who initially didn't have the luxury of a big name to sell. FaBrizio talks about the interesting dynamics. "We would go to a trade show and you would see nine out of ten distributors doing their expenses (at their booth) and people still bought from them because they had a big name."

People bought from Simple Green for a different reason. Over the years, the company has proven to keep its brand promise of safety, efficiency and simplicity of use. The product is available everywhere from air shows to home improvement shows. One woman known as "the Lawn and Garden Lady" from Chicago orders 15,000 samples from them every single year. FaBrizio says, "Stack that up against thirty years and you have a big contingency of users from car clubs to little leagues to soccer fields."

In 1985, when a company tried to acquire Simple Green, they did a blind study as part of their due diligence. "If you give someone a sample and 40 percent of the time they buy it, it's a home run," says FaBrizio. "Colgate was interested in buying Simple Green because our conversion was 78 percent."

So why doesn't a large corporation just duplicate what Simple Green has done? "A product launch is costly and a product recall can cost an entire division their jobs," says FaBrizio. "They're better off finding companies with tremendous loyalty. That's what built our brand."

And Simple Green has been loyal to every customer from the U.S. Government to the little league moms who use it. They have consistently delivered even under the most extreme circumstances.

"We did a lot of homework early on. We had data on the disbursement of oil into the ocean years before the Exxon Valdez incident happened," says FaBrizio. When the Exxon Valdez did strike Bligh Reef, spilling more than 11 million gallons of crude oil in Prince William Sound Alaska, Simple Green was there to help. The spill was the largest in U.S. history, complicated by the remote location only accessible by helicopter and boat. Says FaBrizio, "We were on every Coast Guard ship in Alaska. We've built a reputation of truthfulness, quality and integrity."

"We're never the cheapest; normally we're the most expensive. Big companies want you to fill your shopping cart with their cleaning products. With Simple Green, you just need one or two products to clean your entire house." They also provide concentrated products – users can add their own water – it makes for a more cost effective product.

Simple Green is still getting the attention of major corporations who now want to clean up their act. "We've been invited by the president of Wal-Mart to help them 'green up,'" he says. "Wal-Mart generated the largest amount of retail waste in the world." Simple Green is now working with the $312 billion a year company to support their efforts to become a more environmentally efficient corporation.

Now, in their 32nd year of operation, Simple Green is still considered a small competitor to Clorox and Procter and Gamble. "Our ad budget is dwarfed by our competitors," he says. "I spend as much on advertising in one year as P&G does in one day. Our PR portion is more visible because they go hand in hand." Simple Green's PR component is the EGBAR foundation. EGBAR (an acronym for his earlier mantra of Everything's Going to Be All Right) is dedicated to educating children throughout the world about the importance of protecting the environment and creating a greater environmental awareness of community clean up needs. Simple Green gives a percentage of sales to these causes. They have partnered with the Catalina Island Conservancy, raising over $3 million for the cause, which protects 42,000 acres and 50 miles of shoreline, a botanical garden nature center and more than 200 miles of roads. EGBAR has also been a part of SEA Lab, a Southern California Edison Marine Research Laboratory which provides state of the art fish protection systems. The USS EGBAR, an interactive education program based in a submarine themed kiosk, launched its maiden voyage in 2005 to help visitors of the SEA Lab understand how waste disposal harms the environment and how recycling can help.

The **EBGAR** Foundation is a significant and pervasive way for their primary company to reinforce the product brand. FaBrizio says, "We show how one person at a time can have an impact. We've done it for 20 plus years. We've adopted five miles of California's Huntington Beach Coastline. We've paid 15 non profit groups $1500 each year to clean up the beaches each month. We sponsor the number one bicycle team in California - 300 Simple Green Jerseys are worn by the bikers who ride throughout Orange County."

Because of FaBrizio's dedication to his product and his cause, he never had to rely on fads. Its funny how doing the right thing can actually be good for business. And as long as FaBrizio is keeping an eye on his company and the environment, there's a good chance everything's going to be all right.

The Greening of Corporate America

Whether motivated by the good intentions or the bottom line, more companies are finding ways to go green.

Wal-Mart has set goals to increase efficiency of its vehicle fleet by 25 percent over the next three years and double efficiency in ten years; eliminate 30 percent of energy used in stores; reduce solid waste from U.S. stores by 25 percent in three years and invest $500 million in sustainability products. They are currently the largest seller of organic milk and the biggest buyer of organic cotton in the world.

Dupont has decreased greenhouse gas emissions by 72 percent since 1990 and reduced global energy use 9 percent, for $3 billion in savings.

GE will reduce greenhouse gas emissions one percent by 2012 – without this commitment, the emissions would have increased by 40 percent by 2012.

Goldman Sachs will put $1 billion into clean energy investments and will purchase more local products.

INTEL will reduce greenhouse gas emissions by 10 percent of 1995 levels.

UPS has developed a 1500 alternative fuel fleet and has ordered 50 hybrid electric delivery trucks which will cut fuel consumption by 44,000 gallons in one year.

McDonalds, in partnership with **Environmental Defense (formerly Environmental Defense Fund)** is changing their refrigeration equipment to reduce emissions of green house gasses *and* reduce refrigeration costs by 17 percent.

Target is the only national retailer with a hanger reuse program, reusing them 92 percent of the time, keeping 376 million hangers out of landfills. Once hangers exceed their useful life, Target recycles them for other uses like flower pots and plastic silverware. In 2005, they recycled 2.3 million pounds of plastic. The corporation also has targeted efforts to recycle shrink-wrap, cardboard, obsolete electronics, and shopping carts.

Brandstorming Questions

1. Is a green strategy appropriate for my company? Consider the costs and changes necessary to make a green strategy work. You will have to determine the return on investment (ROI).

2. Is the strategy something that can be used as a differentiator? Keep in mind, that doing something that is good for the environment is only a differentiator if your competitors are not doing it and if it is tied into your primary offering. Otherwise, it is a component of your company's social responsibility program.

Strategy # 19:

Create a brand experience

Business Development Institute - *www.bdionline.com*

If your clients could experience your brand, what would it feel like? What senses would be touched? What emotions? What rational or cultural messages would resonate with them? Many companies talk about their brands, but Guy Alvarez, founder of the Business Development Institute (BDI) helps companies give their prospects a true brand experience.

"We specialize in experiential marketing," says Alvarez. "We help prospects to experience a company's brand and help the prospect know what it would be like to do business with that company." BDI achieves this through their trademarked Wingspan development platform which goes beyond just event planning by incorporating research, specific business goals and detailed follow up to determine return on investment.

The idea came when Alvarez and his partner Steve Etzler, both former KPMG business development professionals, realized there was no group or network of business development executives to help them generate new leads. They came up with the concept of BDI and invited people to attend regularly scheduled meetings for free as long as attendees met the qualifications. In the process of conducting the meetings, they were approached by a large management consulting firm who wanted them to do the same type of meetings for their financial services group. "We then realized that relationships are the core to any business," says Alvarez, and BDI became an official company.

"Experiential marketing is already a hot concept in the business to consumer world, where companies do road tours and get the mass consumer audience to experience a particular product," says Alvarez. "But in the business to business world, it's tougher because a company may be trying to sell a prospect on hiring their firm to provide a particular service, not just on sampling a tangible product."

BDI has an impressive client list. They created a year-long business development program for Microsoft. The technology giant wanted to target senior executives at upper middle market companies - defined as those companies with 500 to 1500 personal computers. Microsoft wanted to target these companies to showcase their products in development that would meet the needs of this group.

Microsoft's strategy had always been similar to most companies – focus on features and benefits. But Alvarez's research revealed that senior executives are more interested in high level business issues such as security and productivity. He recalls, "We developed a kick-off event at the Rainbow Room in New York, focused on teamwork and leadership. We hired Super Bowl MVP, Phil Simms, formerly of the New York Giants, to speak about teamwork and leadership through the eyes of a football player." Needless to say, Simms scored big with the male demographic.

More than 150 CEOs attended the event. After the keynote, Microsoft spoke briefly about their roadmap of products and services as it related to the audience. They also showcased products that would enable teamwork and leadership. The event generated a significant amount of new business for Microsoft and was deemed so successful, that BDI now does monthly events based on key topics developed in concert with Microsoft.

The experiences BDI provides are primarily live events, staying true to the belief that live interaction with your target audience is crucial. "Shake hands, develop a trusting relationship," Alvarez says – something that is often forgotten in the high speed, high tech business to business world.

Another satisfied BDI client was the City of Amsterdam, whose representatives were targeting New York City business leaders considering setting up offices in Europe.

BDI first created an online survey that asked each business representative questions about their expansion plans and time frames. BDI contributed $25 to a charity for each survey completed as an incentive to increase participation. The strategy to get individuals to participate in the survey got the attention of leading marketing blogs, who wrote of the genius of their plan.

Based on survey responses, BDI created a golf event. With seventy people in attendance, the City of Amsterdam's representatives did a presentation on the advantages of setting up shops in their city and brought in a company who did it successfully, making a compelling argument on the merits of Amsterdam as a business hub. Cocktails and networking followed – so did numerous leads and meetings with representatives for the City of Amsterdam.

Other clients included a leading executive recruitment firm, Solomon Page group, who has a legal division in New York and contracts temporary to permanent attorneys. Rather than host a large public event, BDI created a private dinner series at Per Se, one of New York's most exclusive restaurants. The top litigator from the Enron trial spoke to and audience including forty of the top litigators in New York. The event was so successful, it is now an ongoing dinner series branded as the "Litigators Platinum Roundtable."

After each event, BDI follows up with attendees to schedule meetings between them and the client. In some cases, clients prefer to do the contacts themselves. Either way, BDI stresses the importance of post event follow up in an organized manner. It's an important measurement of new business development and return on investment.

So what type of investment and what type of return can a company expect? Microsoft has more than quadrupled their investment dollars.

Alvarez points out the difference between what he does in comparison to a general public relations firm. "PR companies do events, but we focus on the target audience. We become creative and strategic in how we're going to deliver to the audience."

And Alvarez practices what he preaches, hosting events for BDI as well.

After all, living your own brand is the best way to turn prospects into believers. Alvarez states, "We believe in our services. As a way to have people we are working with understand the quality of events we create, we conduct our own special events and generate new business for ourselves. We developed a network in New York of more than 20,000 senior level executives." With only ten employees, Alvarez has been able to leverage the power of influential executives and help change their business experiences from high tech to high touch.

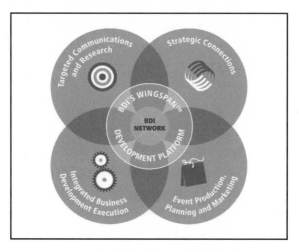

The BDI Wingspan platform encompasses more than just events. They use an integrated system of research, planning and follow through which sets them apart from special events companies.

Brandstorming Questions

1. What is the experience that people have with my brand? (you can refer back to your original grid)
   a. Visual
   b. Emotional
   c. Rational
   d. Cultural

2. If I cannot define an experience that is associated with my company, how can I create an experience?

   a. Short term experiences might include special events, interactive websites, games, blogs, etc.
   b. Long term experiences might include regular educational programs, support groups, anniversary celebrations, and ongoing company traditions.

Strategy # 20:

Give your brand an extreme makeover

(but only if the situation warrants)

VISTAGE™
better leaders • decisions • results

Vistage International (formerly TEC International) - *www.vistage.com*

If you had an organization with fifty years of established success, more than 13,000 members, and a presence in fifteen countries, would you change your brand? Vistage Chief Marketing Officer, Laura DiPietro did. So I had only one question for her. Why?

Vistage, formerly TEC International, was formed in 1957 when Wisconsin businessman Robert Nourse met with four Chief Executive Officers in the Milwaukee Valve Company to challenge each other and make recommendations to help each other's businesses grow. Originally branded TEC (The Executive Committee), the spirit of those meetings continues to the present day.

TEC members have monthly meetings worldwide, keynote speakers, retreats, individual coaching and a global network of professionals with whom they can share their best practices. The sole motivation for members is to help each other's businesses grow. And the system works. TEC claims that their members are more successful than their non-TEC counterparts and, on average, grow their revenues at twice the percentage growth rate after joining the organization.

But change was inevitable for the TEC brand because something else had changed since those early meetings in 1957 - something that Nourse himself could have never imagined. DiPietro explains, "The repositioning of technology as an industry in the eighties and nineties made our name become very confusing, misleading and seen as a disadvantage in our industry because people thought we were in the high-tech business. Our name became outdated." And DiPietro would now have to begin the process of changing a global brand. But where do you begin?

With twenty-five years of marketing experience, a bachelor's degree in international relations from the University of California, Davis, an MBA from Pepperdine University, and two corporate name changes under her belt, DiPietro was up for the challenge. But to those of you who are considering changing your brand, I caution you that this definitely falls in the "don't try this at home" category, unless you are a brand guru or are working with a skilled agency with a proven track record in branding.

DiPietro began a collaborative effort with two such agencies, keeping involved in all phases of the process. She states, "I emphasize that as you go through the branding process, there has to be a person with ownership from the company who is driving it, passionate about it, and living it, to make it work."

Her first task was to get buy in from all stakeholders. In the case of this membership organization, the stakeholders included three diverse groups – 13,000 members, 500 chairs and 600 speakers – all with different perspectives on what TEC meant to them.

DiPietro and her team relied heavily on input from the key constituents as they negotiated their way through the re-branding maze; however, they began with one non-negotiable point. The new name should be invented – not a common word that had been previously used. This would enable them to avoid trademark issues and to create an original brand with no associations or baggage.

DiPietro recalls, "We wanted something that was made up and very clean from a global and online aspect. We crafted the name – based on descriptors of what we stand for and what we deliver to our members. Vistage is a combination of 'vista' referring to a higher perspective and 'advantage' referring to the advantage gained through a better vision of what needs to happen in your business."

The group ruled out one suggested name 'Everest' because it was not a unique name and already had trademarks in other industries. Another option, Navex – which represented navigating from a higher point – was a valid contender, but had a harder sound. "Vistage was easier on the ear. You have to get granular on the name for it to play well in your arena," says DiPietro.

Barriers to acceptance from key stakeholders and the importance of their level of commitment to championing the brand were also considered. "We assessed each group individually," DiPietro recalls. "The members were okay with it once we presented the logic behind it. Our members are progressive people – they understood it. The most difficult part of this group was the older members who viewed TEC as something steeped in tradition, which is understandable."

The TEC Chairs were a challenge. Chairs are responsible for leading the monthly groups and recruiting new members. "We took a lot of time to educate them, survey them, hold focus groups, and engaged the chair community in giving us feedback through the process. We had advisory board meetings with color schemes, logos, taglines, and feedback. When we did roll it out, they could be proud of it and stand behind it – even if some didn't like it – they could still philosophically support it. We spent a lot of time and money and effort in the interactive process. The speakers were the easiest to engage because most speakers are independent people, life learners, adaptable, accepting of change and it was very well received."

Another tactic was to create a brand book which they sent out to chairs, members, and staff. DiPietro recalls, "We took people through it in a fun way and created excitement around what was to come. We communicated it in a more marketing sense. It was well received and was done in October, far in advance of the public announcement in May."

The new name rollout included a direct mail campaign to constituents consisting of gift boxes with Vistage branded gifts. A T-shirt, mug, luggage tags and an informational letter on the new name and rationale behind it arrived in a box with the new Vistage signature colors of sky blue and white, giving it a fresh, streamlined look. Accompanying press releases to the media and messaging on the old and new websites completed the transition.

Most often, a seamless transition is covering a complex execution. I believe that the original members of The Executive Committee would have been proud that the collaborative process they put in place more than half a century ago, is still applied today by the organization's members and leaders whose job is to keep the brand engaging and relevant through this century and beyond.

Brandstorming Questions

1. Is my brand in need of a makeover?

2. Is my brand outdated?
   a. Visually – logo, graphics, colors
   b. Messaging – are taglines or messages outdated because new terminology has become available or has time changed the meaning of the terminology I am using?
   c. Is my company's technology outdated – computers, customer relationship management systems, website interface? What can I do to improve this?

3. If my brand is in need of a makeover, am I willing to commit the time to making sure I do this correctly?

4. Which experts can I call on to help me through this process?

5. What new image would I like to project? What would I want to achieve as a result of the change?

6. Who are the key stakeholders that must be involved in the process? How can I communicate the benefit to them?

8. How much am I willing to contribute in terms of time, revenue and human resources to make this happen?

Bold Approach

www.boldapproach.com / www.howtopersuade.com

You could ask Dave Lakhani about his business, but he's just going to tell you a story. He's not being nostalgic, he's actually employing one of the oldest methods of persuasive communication, used since the days of folklore. And he's teaching his clients to do the same. Story telling is back in a big way as one of the hottest trends in marketing. And there's no better person than Lakhani to teach others how to profit from the craft.

A published author, professional speaker and business consultant specializing in the art of persuasion, Lakhani's own story began when his mother brought him and his two brothers to a place that would ultimately teach him about the power of persuasion - a religious cult. In his book, *Persuasion: The Art of Getting What You Want* (Wiley, 2005), Lakhani recalls those days:

> When it was time for punishment, there was no sparing the rod or spoiling the child. One of my younger brothers suffered terribly during those years. He has what would likely now be diagnosed as attention deficit disorder and what has since tested as a very high IQ. The leaders of the church diagnosed him as "having the Devil in him," and prescribed regular beatings to get the Devil out of him...What amazed me most as I grew older, was the number of people that unquestioningly accepted this story I've just told you without question. Many of these people were well educated and from well-adjusted homes,

though not all. Day after day, year after year, those very same people willingly gave up much of what they earned to support a minister (to whom many of the rules didn't apply) and a church, all while spreading the good work and attracting even more people to the church and drawing them in systematically until they, too, were completely hooked.

The experience taught Lakhani about the abuse of persuasion from the experts – cult leaders. Their methods achieved desired results for them but were horrific in their execution and impact, using manipulation, deception and violence to initially persuade and ultimately control others. Lakhani's interest in the subject grew after he left the cult and became determined to teach others how to persuade through legitimate and ethical means.

When it comes to using persuasion in branding, Lakhani sets the record straight. "It's important to recognize a couple of things. First, you are not your logo. That's where some people get confused about a brand. Brand only exists in the mind of the consumer. If you understand what happens in the prospect's mind, body, and psychology during persuasion, you'll have some indication of how it can be used in communicating your brand and creating the client's brand experience."

Storytelling can keep your brand in your prospect's mind long after you've left them. Lakhani says, "People buy into stories – they like the idea that they're part of something bigger than themselves, they put themselves into the scene; that is the experience. When you tell the story of you, you're positioning yourself differently from everything else and you are engaging them deeply, emotionally."

Lakhani's message is echoed by marketing experts like Seth Godin, who says that successful marketers don't talk about features and benefits; instead they tell us a story that we want to believe. Lakhani explains, "People remember good stories – and they pass them on to others. How many times have your friends come to you and exuberantly rattled off a list of features and benefits of their favorite product? More likely, they've come to you with a great story about the product, how they enjoyed it; how it made them feel; what it meant to them. They told you a story. And perhaps it was enough to get you to try the product."

Lakhani says, "in telling the story of who I am and how my mom raised her three sons in a cult, I am able to communicate my understanding of how people will respond to specific applications of persuasion. People are more impacted by story and metaphor - they can remember them easier."

A professional speaker, Lakhani has presented to about 100,000 people from "Bombay to Boise" as he says. He has worked with every type of professional – salesmen, lawyers and politicians who are looking to persuade more effectively. He has helped legal organizations to better persuade juries and government agencies to position messages more effectively.

Lakhani recalls helping a specific client - a financial planner – with the art of storytelling to improve his practice. You'll probably agree that while many people need financial planners, few can articulate a strong point of differentiation among them. Lakhani's client was a successful executive, closing two out of every five sales calls, using the same pitch as other financial planners. He could have continued on that path and done very well, but remember, differentiation is about gaining a competitive advantage, not competitive parity. And that advantage came to the professional when Lakhani taught him the power of story telling.

Lakhani recalls, "We took his story apart. I learned that when he was young, he watched his father go to work every day. One day, dad came home and sat the family down around the table. He had been laid off. The family had no money or savings and was only a few checks away from being destitute. It impacted him in a big way. He knew then that he would have to learn to handle money and accumulate wealth. He became very astute at learning how to invest and ultimately turned $1000 into $1 million in under a year. From a powerful experience at age 15 that left him feeling helpless and embarrassed, he emerged as a person who took control so the painful experience could never happen again. And this story would become a part of his next sales call."

Lakhani explains the remarkable results. "Since implementing the storytelling technique, the executive has closed 100 percent of all deals which at the present time includes a significant number of new clients. He also has been able to give the story a successful resolution – he has helped his father manage and grow his money, moving him to a place of financial security."

Stories help people become committed to brands – almost in a cult like way. Of course, the word cult and the experience Lakhani had was a negative one, but there are positive cult brands. "Harley Davidson is a cult brand –once someone is committed to the brand, they don't have to think anymore – they don't have to consider other brands – they've discovered salvation. It changes from being a choice to being a core belief. Once you align with a core belief, you don't have to think about a choice anymore." This can be done with a well built brand. You can see core beliefs in many brands. People buy Chevy's or Ford's, Mercedes or BMW's. People become brand loyal once they identify with the brand and have the right experience while using the brand.

"The right experience is beyond words," he says. "Motivate them (your clients) in a way that's more meaningful than they could possibly tell you," says Lakhani. And that message is helping Lakhani's clients create their own happy endings.

Brandstorming Questions

1. Does my company have a story that creates a difference in the mind of the consumer – perhaps my company started based on a strong conviction of the founders to do things differently?

2. Did my company begin because of a discovery or new innovation? Am I telling the story or is it just a page on my website? How can I best leverage this story to set myself apart?

3. How can my sales team use their own unique stories to sell themselves to the client?

4. Am I willing to work with my sales team and staff to make sure they are telling a consistent story in a compelling manner?

Community Bank Ventures - *www.communitybankventures.com*

In the rapid pace of today's business, to stand still is to fall behind. By combining the high rates of return on community bank investments with a strategy to capture the emerging Hispanic market, Community Bank Ventures is moving forward with a plan that will create tremendous value for all stakeholders.

The Hispanic population is the fastest growing ethnic group in the United States today. Between 1980 and the present, the number of Hispanics in the U.S. grew by 53 percent compared to 68 percent for the U.S. population, and now represents 13.5 percent of Americans. Combine those numbers with another emerging trend – traditional community banking - and you have an opportunity to leverage powerful statistics and fulfill a community need. Community Bank Ventures is doing just that.

Traditional community banks strengthen a community's economic standing in two ways; by reinvesting in the community and presenting an attractive investment opportunity for local investors. Community bank shareholders can have a direct impact on the bank's success by doing business there. And community members benefit from economic support that can lead to the area's long term development and vitality.

Community Bank Ventures has drilled down further to find specific areas of need for community banking in the Hispanic market. Cesar Rosas,

Executive Vice President, Director of Emerging Bank Markets shares the details of the research that helped the firm reveal a market in Riverside, California that was ripe for entry:

- Out of 50 states, California ranks first in bank deposits, but 50th in bank branches per capita.

- Population per bank branch in the U.S. is 3,220; in Riverside, California, it is 6,801.

- The city's bank deposits have grown by 43 percent or $1 billion in the last three years.

- Riverside was ranked as the second best place to do business in America by *Inc.* Magazine

- The population is 45 percent Hispanic.

The facts helped Community Bank Ventures define a market and a strategy; and they are just as diligent about reaching the market as they were about defining it.

Rosas explains that many community banks are attractive acquisition targets for larger banks. This dynamic has consistently bolstered the value of community banks and provided significant returns to investors. "For every 2.8 bank mergers and acquisitions, there is only 1 new bank." These acquisitions are an indicator that larger banks clearly see the return on investment of the community banks, but once acquired, community members miss an opportunity to provide sound returns for founders, organizers, directors, and shareholders – and in this case the Hispanic market in the community of Riverside.

Jeff Rigsby, President and CEO of Community Bank Ventures says, "Rosas' first order of business will be to initiate three new bank projects with an emphasis on serving the Hispanic business owner and their employees." The project will involve raising $12 to $15 million in capital per project, much of which will come from local business leaders and the proposed banks' board of directors. Rosas says, "Each person should ideally have a vested interest – not just because of the generous returns from investing in the bank, but for the positive impact it will have on community members and business owners." But to make it successful, the bank will have to know how to create a brand that will capture the complex and diverse Hispanic community. And reaching the Hispanic market often involves methods that larger banks are not willing or able to act on.

Rosas says, "Running a bank in a Hispanic market entails more than just having bilingual employees. There must be an understanding of the culture and how Hispanics do business," he says. The trust factor comes when the clients feel that their needs are understood from a cultural level that goes beyond the language.

Rosas states, "Community banks fill the void that big banks can't fill. We will have four to five business development officers who will build relationships over the long term with local Hispanic business owners." Part of the process is getting to know the client – not just rushing in. He says, "We might have several meetings with the customer and get to know him and his family before ever doing business with them." And by taking care of clients, they're taking care of investors.

Rosas explains. "In addition to providing historically attractive returns, community banks present a relatively lower risk than other investments. Community banks are held to high standards and regulations set by federal and state agencies." Community banks are also more tightly regulated in the first three years. During that time, an officer or board member replacement requires authorization from regulators. Rosas says, "Out of 1456 community banks that formed in the US between 1990 and 2004, only four failed. Of those four, none were from California." Community banks have shown returns as high as 60 percent over a three year period and nearly 400 percent over a ten year period.

The business model will be a win-win for the residents of Riverside and for those investors who helped facilitate the bank's growth. The attention to dealing with a specific market type will be a major contributing factor for the bank's success. Rosas says, "The bank wants to share the vision with the client- it's our biggest competitive advantage."

Other Emerging Markets in Community Banking

Immigrant Banking – As immigrants to America achieve business success they also realize the need to have banks that understand their cultural needs.

Faith Based Banking – Many religious and interfaith groups believe that helping the poor means creating better communities, not just giving donations. These groups are bringing their beliefs into play to change lives by investing in their respective communities through community banks.

Islamic Banking - There are now thirty Islamic banks in operation outside of Iran and Pakistan and the numbers are growing significantly.

Native American Banking - A presidential executive order on "Consultation and Coordination with Indian Tribal Governments" (November 6, 2000), has enabled the OCC to work with federally acknowledged Indian tribes for the formation of a bank.

Brandstorming Questions

1. What emerging markets can be identified in my industry?

    a. Ethnic

    b. Demographic

    c. Socioeconomic

    d. Gender

    e. Age

    f. Other

2. In which emerging market am I willing to invest?

    a. Time

    b. Money

    c. Staffing and Staff training to deal with these markets

    d. Promotions

    e. Other

Velázquez

Velázquez Press - *www.velazquezpress.com* / *www.askvelazquez.com*

"Spanish is my language.

English, I grew up with.

To express, I speak both."

The quote is featured on a poster designed to resonate with the bilingual Spanish American who lives between two worlds but feels very much a part of both. Velázquez Press is bridging the communication and cultural needs of those who speak Spanish as a primary language but want to become proficient in English.

Velázquez has been recognized throughout the world as the preeminent authority in Spanish and English dictionaries for more than 150 years. In 2003, Academic Learning Company acquired *Velázquez Spanish and English Dictionary*. Velázquez Press is committed to developing new bilingual dictionaries for children, students and adults and is building their business one relationship at a time.

Spanish is the second most common language in the United States after English. According to the 2000 United States Census, Spanish is spoken most frequently at home by about 28.1 million people aged five or over. Of these, 14.3 million reported that they also spoke English "Very well." If words were all that was necessary to learn a language, there would be no need for a publisher to consider culture. But Velázquez Press knows that culture is an important part of communication. And their branding shows that they've entered the marketplace with more than just words.

The company has built a reputation on incorporating culture into their brand. "The language is a reflection of the people and culture," says Daniel Morales, Communications Director of Velázquez Press. "We understand the branding of the dictionary for teaching purposes - teaching people about the language, the expression of people and cultures. So when we do the marketing we build emotion into the name by building cultural events within the bilingual community."

But not all businesses are ready to merge with other cultures. When this happens, Morales is there to enlighten them. The legendary Geno's Steaks in Philadelphia is one company that received a first hand lesson in biculturalism from the people at Velázquez. It seems the legendary Phili Cheesesteaks eatery known as "the best in South Phili" had a sign in their window where customers place their order. It read,

---

"This is America.
When ordering, speak English."

Aside from the obvious - people who can't speak English can't read English – it was a sign that Geno's may not have done their marketing homework. If they did, they would have a better understanding of their changing patron mix. Philadelphia's demographics have been transforming from a predominantly white population in 1990, to a significant minority-mixed in 2000. The change occurred as increases in African Americans, Hispanics, and Asians were coupled with an 180,000-person decline in white residents. Foreign-born residents in the city increased by 34,000 in the 1990's and more than twice that number settled in the suburbs over the same period of time. These groups include individuals from Southeast Asia, Eastern Europe, and the Caribbean.

Yet, the city's resistance to a melding of these cultures is palpable - different ethnic groups tend to live in separate areas of the city; and the City of Brotherly Love ranks the highest in the nation on segregation between whites and Hispanics. It seems the sign in the window at Geno's is indicative of a much bigger issue.

Morales sent the *Velázquez Spanish and English Dictionary* to Geno's owner Joseph Vento, along with a letter encouraging him to use the book to help his staff communicate with their growing population of non-English speaking patrons.

Morales stated in a press release about the incident, "Mr. Vento is a son of immigrants and his appreciation for the English language is unparalleled. The issues at hand are communication and the challenges of human integration in a modern world where a foreign land is a short plane ride away and people who primarily speak other languages are living the American experience themselves."

Morales says of the situation "it's not about English only issues," he says "First people need to understand this community." He refers to a recent incident that occurred on KCPW Radio during a Republican primary radio debate. Congressional challenger John Jacob used an anti-Hispanic statement to gain leverage with incumbent Chris Canon whom he felt was being soft on immigration issues. Jacob stated, "These people (Hispanics) have come into America without permission and they've brought diseases, they've brought all kinds of things."

"He didn't understand," says Morales. "When we understand each other, then we can accept each other and build a community together. When it comes to doing business with people, that's very important – to be successful, you have to understand their particular needs. A lot of companies coming out are addressing the cultural needs of people – foods, flavors, clothing, items for their homes; they are actually becoming successful by understanding purchasing behavior."

Velázquez stays close to prospects by hosting Bilingual Nights. The events are held throughout the country and are not a hard sell for the dictionary – they are an opportunity to bring their core market together. The poster mentioned earlier was created for these events and demonstrates an understanding of issues within the bilingual community. Morales says, "If you are in a bilingual family, some things can only be expressed in English, some can only be expressed in Spanish. The events engage students and audiences with books, authors, and musicians. We bring them together to discuss bilingualism in a space where they're able to talk about issues that impact them - things like growing up speaking Spanish in an English school."

Events can vary depending on the area. For example, media events might include local TV stations, music festivals, or cultural events like Cinco de Mayo (the fifth of May), a Mexican holiday which celebrates the Mexican victory over French occupation in 1862. Smaller events with the same format are done at book stores and libraries. Posters of the dictionaries are at the events, but that's the only marketing that exists. Velázquez also offers a website, (*www.askvelazquez.com*) not to sell products but to post messages, ask questions and maintain a community. The events are growing and vary depending on the area. Morales says, "We're getting more and more involved with high profile events like working with the Latin Grammy's, and the Palm Beach Film Festival. After the events, we will do a party with a message of the communication between the Spanish and English speaking world."

Morales promotes the importance of a global mindset. He says, "Promoting a monolingual culture would be a mistake. As a Spanish and English reference dictionary we want to position ourselves ahead of the game."

Competitors haven't copied them yet, most focus on electronic versions of their dictionaries and various technological features. "We try to build an emotional association, versus the competition who focuses on how fast they can search for a word. We do those things, but don't focus on it as part of the brand."

This statement is key – just because you do something, doesn't mean it has to be a part of your brand message. In this case, developing a cultural bond with the customer is a much harder brand element to imitate than the technology component promoted by their competitors. Velázquez has the technology; but its competitors do not have the relationships.

The competition might take a lesson from Velázquez. It is now estimated that Hispanic buying power in the U.S. is $700 billion annually and will climb to $1 trillion by 2010. While some might think holding special events and building relationships is a slower way of getting business, it's a process that shows an understanding of a culture that favors relationships first, business second.

The events and websites are decidedly public relations, not sales functions, but the relationships built over time will bode well for sales. Morales says, "You don't want to sell anything – you want people to buy. We create an atmosphere for people to associate with. When they need a dictionary they will buy it from us."

Challenges & Considerations in Marketing to Hispanics

- The Hispanic market has a variety of segments, each with its own buying patterns and needs that could impact marketing approach:
    - Mexicans 66.9 %
    - Central & South Americans 14.3 %
    - Puerto Ricans 8.6 %
    - Cubans 3.7 %

- Hispanics who have lived in the U.S. for a short period of time have different buying patterns than those who have lived in the U.S. for several generations, the former tending to purchase in small, urban stores, the latter, retail chains.

- Customer sophistication varies. A product sold at a discounter like Wal-Mart in the U.S., may be considered a high end brand in Latin America.

- Hispanics often live in younger, larger families that are more likely to live in multigenerational households than the general U.S. population.

- Hispanic families are more likely to make purchasing decisions as a group, often doing things like grocery shopping or banking together.

- Tend to be brand loyal and respond to Hispanic spokespersons.

- Newer immigrants often do not have established lines of credit or their own credit cards.

- Densely populated Hispanic groups, such as Mexicans living in Los Angeles, may be more likely to hold on to their own culture and less likely to assimilate into American culture, than Hispanics in areas where their population is more dispersed.

- Researching buying patterns may be difficult because many Hispanics shop in small, inner city stores that do not scan items. This data would have to be tracked manually.

Brandstorming Questions

1. Is there a cultural market that my company can target?

2. What barriers does this market currently have to accessing my services?

    a. Lack of understanding about my business?

    b. Language barriers?

    c. No current communications to this market from my company?

    d. Lack of understanding on my company's part on how to approach this market?

    e. Inability of my staff to work with the special needs of this market?

3. How much am I able to invest in targeting this market? What are the benefits? Are my competitors addressing this market? If not, can this be my company's point of differentiation?

Strategy # 24:

Be Strange

The Church of Tom Jones

www.churchoftomjones.com

www.pulc.com

Whenever two or more are gathered, Pastor Jack Stahl will preach the gospel of "peace, love and an abundant life" at the Church of Tom Jones. But before you rush to pelt your panties at the pulpit, be warned his messages are far from traditional, often including powerful expletives. (As the great niece of a Pentecostal minister, I felt compelled to furnish this disclaimer right up front).

At the age of six, Stahl witnessed Tom Jones' 1969 television debut and was forever changed. Like many viewers, he was mesmerized by Tom's voice and gyrations. "It made me feel as if I was surrounded by angels," he recalls.

So it was only natural that after his calling to the ministry in 1990, he would incorporate the music of the inspirational Welshman into his preaching. And, after attending more than 200 Tom Jones concerts, this man of the cloth (the cloth, in this case, being leather pants worn by Stahl during his services) has the songs and the moves that give his ministry a point of differentiation that you just don't see every Sunday.

Jack grew up Catholic and only occasionally attended church. When he finally decided to go into the ministry, he believed it was because he needed to "give the word in a way that people needed to hear it." He explains that the expletives are a necessary means by which to cast out the devil, who can sense cowardice.

"God called me into this for what I can bring and I'm not editing. I'm not for everyone. I show people that when dealing with the devil you've got to be tough – you've got to stand tall. Satan is like a schoolyard bully, and the only way to handle this coward is to stand up to him and say, 'You're not gonna take my f-ing milk money anymore!' Many people would not respond to me without this strong message. There are a lot of people that are attracted to the straightforwardness of my communication. I can appeal to people that someone else might not be able to."

Another departure from the traditional is Pastor Jack's use of technology to get his word out to the masses. In addition to his personal visits with people all over the country to perform marriages, baptisms, funerals and exorcisms, the pastor preaches through his radio ministry, broadcast each day to a congregation of 100,000. He also has two websites, pod casts and even a Tom Jones Exorcism Hotline. Pastor Jack reasons, "Can you imagine the wear and tear Jesus would have saved on his feet if he had access to the Internet?"

Most of the church's revenues are generated from offerings of spiritual degrees, diplomas, and ordination programs by mail. For a donation, you can become a Legally Ordained Minister. Other certificates are awarded for life, work or educational experience. "We ordain anyone that believes in peace, love and an abundant life. Many people want to start their own ministry. A lot of churches say 'we believe in freedom' but they go on to tell you what to believe. I don't tell anyone what to believe. Worship whatever God you believe is your God or higher power. We allow people to worship or not worship as they choose and they love the freedom."

And they undoubtedly love the price. For only $19.50, you can receive a certificate of ordainment and a wallet card. Other offerings include Bronze, Silver, Gold or Platinum Partner Ministerial packages which contain instructional manuals, marriage certificates, press/clergy dashboard plates and Doctorate of Divinity or Doctor of Philosophy Certifications. Depending on the level, these packages can range between $94 and $1800, but at the time of this writing were on sale for as much as 70 percent off.

And before you dismiss strangeness and controversy as a valid brand strategy, consider the benefits. Pastor Jack has been featured on more than 100 radio and television programs in seven countries including VH1, the Ricki Lake Show and the BBC. In 1997 he was dubbed "The Strangest Person in America" by the nationally syndicated television show, *Strange Universe.* Let's face it – strangeness & controversy are differentiators that can garner significant media attention. They can also create loyal niche markets - Pastor Jack has plans to build a 2500 seat stadium for his followers, giving him yet another venue to showcase offerings and generate revenue for the support of his ministry.

If your business isn't quite right for this type of strategy, don't worry. In the words of the almighty, "it's not unusual."

Divine Differentiation –Pastor Jack has his own special brand of religion.

Brandstorming Questions

1. Could my company benefit from doing the unexpected?

2. If I am in a conservative industry, is there an unusual stance I can take? Some examples might be:

   a. Using humor or irony in advertising.

   b. Providing an unusual experience on my website.

   c. Having a trade show booth or advertisement that sets itself apart in a compelling way such as using images not normally associated with your industry. One automotive company showed a photo of their cars adjacent to photos of faces of people that looked like the car (i.e. photo of a man with big ears was positioned next to a car photographed from the front with its doors opened, to emulate the ears.) The photos of many faces and cars reinforced the point that there is a different car for every person or personality.

Strategy # 25:

Leverage local, regional or national celebrity status

The Lazy Bear Ranch - *www.lazybearranch.com*

Combining his status as a Chicago Bear Super Bowl XX champion, and his love of bird hunting, Tim Wrightman created the "Bears and Birds Weekend" at his Lazy Bear Ranch in Weiser, Idaho. Situated on 150 acres of land in Lewis and Clark territory, the spectacular ranch serves as a "rustic chic" backdrop for guests who come for business, pleasure, or both.

The 5,700 square foot accommodations showcase the creative side of Wrightman who was actively involved in every design element. Treasured accoutrements such as a Super Bowl trophy, and sports and hunting memorabilia adorn cozy rooms which have the comfort of a bed and breakfast, with a rugged charm that appeals to the ranch's largely male demographic. Every room reveals a sports or hunting motif, reminding guests that this will indeed be an adventurous and memorable weekend.

Visitors can hunt a variety of birds, including pheasant, quail, and geese within nine acres of private duck ponds, accompanied by award-winning English Pointers. Fishing is also available for small mouth bass and blue gill, with seasonal salmon excursions along the Weiser River, rated one of the top ten small mouth bass rivers in the country. Cross Country skiing, golfing, boating and horseback packages can also be arranged. And after working up an appetite, guests feast on gourmet meals and adult beverages in the cozy "Bear

Den," equipped with a comfy leather sofa, large screen TV, X Box and DVD player.

But perhaps the most exciting part of the weekend is when guests sit down to watch football along with Tim and at least one of his former Super Bowl XX teammates, who join the group for the weekend – Matt Suey, Tom Thayer, Mike Tomczak, Jim McMahon and, yes, even William "The Fridge" Perry. Now that's an offering that can't be easily imitated.

Repeat business looks promising for the ranch which has only been open to the public for one year. According to Wrightman, "Every client that booked in 2005 is coming back in 2006." Wrightman is not only a good businessman, but a responsible citizen of the idyllic town. "I think all true hunters are conservationists at heart," says Wrightman. "In that respect the Lazy Bear Ranch has been a huge success already. With the help of the Idaho Department of Fish and Game, and the US Fish & Wildlife Service we have recreated acres of wetlands and wildlife habitat."

The ranch is already getting the attention of the media and companies who see it as an ideal retreat for clients and staff. "Operating a ranch is hard work for a city boy," says Wrightman, a Los Angeles native and Chicago resident prior to relocating to his Weiser residence. "But, I love it - even on the long and labor intensive days when it seems like a bad episode of *Green Acres.*"

This bear is anything but lazy – football champ Tim Wrightman has worked diligently to build a brand in sports and in business.*(www.timwrightman.com)*

Brandstorming Questions

1. Do founders of my company have local, regional or national status that I am not leveraging?

2. Are any of my clients prominent people who would be recognized by my prospects and if so, would they give a testimonial to my company via advertising, **PR** or as a direct reference?

3. How can I leverage the celebrity status in events, newsletters, or other communications with clients and prospects?

PEPPERDINE UNIVERSITY
Graziadio School of Business and Management

E2B (Education to Business) Program - *www.Bschool.pepperdine.edu*

The days of the company-funded MBA are rapidly diminishing as fewer corporations offer to cover the cost of their executives' five or six figure advanced degrees. Business schools everywhere are faced with the challenge of making their programs more competitive and relevant than ever before. Pepperdine University's Graziadio School of Business and Management, consistently ranked among the top MBA schools in the U.S. by *Business Week, Forbes, U.S. News & World Report,* and *Financial Times,* has an added element that provides a powerful point of differentiation in the highly competitive B-school market. Their offering creates a win-win-win for students, the university and local businesses.

The Education to Business Program creates partnerships between students and corporations to solve real-world business issues. Doreen Shanahan, a former sales and marketing executive for The Coca-Cola Company, founded the program in 2002 to bring the corporation to the classroom. The students and executives benefit from each others' expertise. The only investment on the part of the business is time and all information shared is highly confidential.

Corporate executives present an issue to the students who work in competing teams to offer solutions based on extensive research, planning and guidance from faculty members. The class thrives on the live case studies; the companies gain a fresh business perspective from students with diverse business backgrounds and career goals.

Shanahan describes the evolution of the applied learning program, "We looked at how we were trying to position ourselves. We reviewed our strategic priorities which included living by our values; enhancing quality through innovative learning; reaching external audiences; and emphasizing relevance and application."

By aligning corporate strategies with marketing initiatives, Shanahan and her colleagues were able to evolve a program which enhanced the Pepperdine brand and created a point of differentiation. "When you look at the competitive landscape, points of parity and of difference, it was important for us to define for a reputable top world business school what real, applied and relevant looks like - inside the classroom and in connecting with businesses outside the classroom. While E2B is a learning methodology, we use it to exemplify one of our brand attributes. It is an extension of our brand – a point of difference."

At the close of the 15-week E2B class case project, the students offer not one, but as many as five solutions in the form of substantial oral and written presentations to the business's key executives. Because students are dealing with real business issues, strict confidentiality is a key program element. The program has resulted in many success stories, but one of the more exciting stories began at the Southern California Alta Dena Dairy, a division of Dean Foods, a multi-billion dollar food and dairy producer, and gave the students a classroom experience they will not likely forget.

Alta Dena contacted the E2B program to develop alternative strategies to reduce or eliminate shrinkage in their plastic milk shipping crates. Shrinkage is a reduction in inventory due to shoplifting, employee theft, paperwork errors or supplier fraud.

Alta Dena was spending millions of dollars a year replacing reusable plastic shipping crates that traveled from their plant to various retail outlets. Shanahan states, "Within a two-year period, Alta Dena's negative fiscal impact had almost doubled to more than $4 million and was approaching $5 million."

Exacerbating the problem were escalating fuel costs which caused resin prices to escalate. The class thoroughly researched the fluid milk market, the competitive and retail landscape, and the micro environment to uncover underlying issues driving the problem.

Guided by detailed research and under the close eye of a highly trained faculty, students continued to peel back the layers of the problem which was more significant in scope than they originally thought. They learned that while Alta Dena was losing a million crates per year, the Southern California dairy industry was losing more than $5 million. The students also learned of shrinkage in other industries that shipped reusable resin containers including the beverage and bakery industries.

"The magnitude of the problems was so great," says Shanahan, "that the milk crates lost by Southern California dairies alone in 2005 if laid end to end, would cover 1541 miles." The length of the state of California.

"Each student group offered different and viable solutions, such as elevating internal awareness to encourage employees to become evangelists for crate recovery," says Shanahan. "To achieve this, 3,000 crates - the average number lost at the plant each week - were stacked in an on-site display, to help employees understand the gravity of the problem. Students also recommended the equation of loss in a meaningful way to employees, which was enough to fund new trucks for the company, or new asphalt for the plant yard. These tactics were intended to make the milk crate issues a part of everyday conversation at the employee and management level."

Other suggestions included the use of one-way packaging, disposable packaging, and the use of radio frequency tracking devices embedded in the crates to close in on the problem. Little did the class know, they were about to do just that. The top of mind awareness created by their research helped one student notice something that might not have otherwise captured his attention.

While driving to work the day after class, one of the students noticed a double-wide tractor trailer loaded with empty milk crates driving on a California freeway. The crates belonged to Alta Dena; the truck did not. He snapped a photo of the truck which was ultimately found to be part of an illegal recycling ring. The class learned that the crates are stolen, recycled and sold back into the market through the supply chain. The student's discovery spurred articles from the *Los Angeles Times*, *The New York Times* and CNBC, who reported that milk crate loss in the dairy industry is an estimated $100 million annually.

The cumulative impact of the discovery and proposed solutions from Pepperdine students was impressive. Shanahan says, "For the first time in four years, Alta Dena has a 10 percent reduction in crate purchases in the last quarter reported."

Pepperdine's Graziadio School E2B program brings academic learning to life. It's just one aspect of the Pepperdine MBA that communicates a powerful point of difference for the school, the students, and the business community. Building a brand means creating a unique and remarkable experience for every client through every detail and every outcome. Because these details and outcomes - good or bad – speak to your clients, they leave impressions in their minds that will remain long after the experience has ended. Shanahan describes this process best when she says, "everything communicates."

The crates belonged to Alta Dena; the truck did not.

Brandstorming Questions

1. How can I create a win-win with my company and key community groups where business synergies exist?

   a. Schools

   b. Churches

   c. Women's Groups

   d. Minority Groups

   e. Environmental Groups

   f. Political Groups

   g. Non competing businesses

   h. Businesses that offer complementary products or services

   i. Other

Strategy # 27:

Build a community

Entreprenuer's Organzation - *www.eonetwork.org*

If Steve Jobs of Apple, Michael Dell of Dell Computers and Ted Leonsis of America Online founded an organization before they became household names, what would it look like? It would look like the Entrepreneurs' Organization (EO). All three were founding members of the non-profit organization which since its inception in 1987 has flourished into a worldwide network of entrepreneurs whose total sales now exceed US $81 billion.

The Entrepreneurs' Organization's strategic vision is to build the world's most influential community of entrepreneurs. Members join to learn and grow through direct peer-to-peer learning, once-in-a-lifetime experiences and connections to experts. EO is designed to provide a more relevant experience than those offered at other professional membership organizations. Global Brand Director Tim Young states, "Our brand has always been for entrepreneurs only. You can join many associations and find hired executives, people that have inherited the family business or those that purchased an existing business rather than built it from scratch. This isn't really a true collection of peers. At the moment we are the only global community solely dedicated to supporting entrepreneurs."

At any given time, approximately 10.1 million adults in the U.S. are attempting to create a new business. Since half these new ventures are started by teams of people, it is estimated that they represent about 5.6 million potential new companies. And the ability for those entrepreneurs to network with like-minded people could have a significant impact on the success of those ventures.

Young explains how the Entrepreneurs' Organization supports this growing market. "We chose a specific mission and vision that resonated with an underserved market segment." Entrepreneurs as a target audience share a similar mentality – they are hungry to learn, focused on the future and very tolerant of risk and change. These qualities help them become successful, but can also isolate them. Imagine you're at a cocktail party worried that you might lose your house and can't make payroll, while your friends are discussing car payments or yard work. An entrepreneur can feel that no one understands or can help them with their particular challenges. "By giving them the opportunity to learn from their peers, EO creates a safe haven for entrepreneurs to grow. Bringing these people together to learn from each other is where our vision differentiates us." So does their entrance criteria. You must join the Entrepreneurs' Organization before your 50th birthday and be the owner, founder or controlling shareholder of a company with annual revenues of $1 million or more.

Even EO's defined values have a more entrepreneurial ring than those of other professional organizations:

- **Boldly Go!—Bet on your own abilities**
- **Thirst for Learning—Be a student of opportunity**
- **Make a Mark—Leave a legacy**
- **Trust and Respect—Build a safe haven for learning and growth**
- **Cool—Create, seek out and celebrate once-in-a-lifetime experiences**

Source: www.eonetwork.org

In addition to monthly chapter meetings that bring EO members together in various cities, members also meet regularly with their forum, a group of 8-10 other entrepreneurs that can grow together for years, building both personal and professional relationships that can last a lifetime. Regional and global events connect members from all over the world. Young states, "We hold a variety of global events in places like Dubai, Washington D.C., Auckland, Marrakesh, San Juan, Kuala Lumpur, and Monterrey. In our 2006/2007 fiscal year, we'll welcome hundreds of members in Lisbon, Colombia, Tokyo and Berlin."

Members participate in once-in-a-lifetime experiences like the Birthing of Giants (BOG) which brings the next generation of entrepreneurial powerhouses to MIT for an intensive training program. Ranked by *Inc.* magazine as the top program of its kind, BOG brings professors from MIT, and Boston and Harvard universities to serve as faculty for the event. The program lasts twelve days per year and spans a three-year period. The group covers the six fundamentals of business including: management, finance, human resources, marketing and sales, operations, and research and development.

The Entrepreneurs' Organization recruits new members at the local chapter level. Young says, "Much of our growth comes from word of mouth – we create a compelling experience that our members really enjoy, and they recommend us to their peers. Our surveys indicate that 94 percent of our members would recommend EO to another business owner." Membership has grown by more than 2,000 members in the last four years, and the organization is currently 6,400 strong with entrepreneurs who employ more than 926,000 workers.

And EO members aren't just making contacts, they're making news. In 2005 alone, twenty-three members and sixteen "E-lumni" made *Inc.* magazine's list of fastest growing companies, an annual report which has featured EO members for years. When asked about competition, Young replied, "as a non- profit, we don't really consider ourselves to be in competition with other organizations or executive education programs. We exist to engage leading entrepreneurs to learn and grow, regardless of the medium that they choose. Indeed, many of our benefits and programs are provided through partnerships with other educational and professional organizations such as

MIT, the Young Presidents' Organization and the World Presidents' Organization."

"It's that adoption of the entrepreneurial mindset, which is driven by our member Board of Directors, that ensures we consistently focus on the needs of our membership and make sure their experience is compelling enough that they keep coming back."

Brandstorming Questions

1. How can my company create a sense of community among prospects? This can include:

   a. Educational events

   b. Networking events

   c. Special events – social, entertainment, the arts

2. How can I use the above to keep clients and prospects engaged over time with my brand and offering?

Strategy # 28:

MBT differentiates with design and technology

MBT® (Masai Barefoot Technology) Physiological Footwear -
www.swissmasaius.com

I recently donated a brand new pair of Nike walking shoes to the Good Will. I had purchased them two weeks earlier and had only worn them a few times. There was nothing wrong with them. They looked good. They performed as they should have. But I could no longer bear to use them because shortly after my purchase, I discovered another shoe – one that made my Nikes seem *so* last millennium. The shoes are called MBT's and if you walked a mile in them, you'd know why I can no longer use any other brand.

MBT may have captured a foothold in the $11.5 billion U.S. athletic footwear market at a crucial time. Growing only 2.8 percent in 2005, the market is clearly mature and in need of an innovative kick start. "If you bring a new innovative product to the market, the consumer is ready to spend the money," according to Adidas Chairman Herbert Hainer. And MBT has combined both athletic and therapeutic innovation into a product that looks like no other.

Even the shape of a product can be a differentiator, but MBT goes a step further with proprietary technology.

The MBT sole is convex, emulating the experience of walking in sand. Each pair of shoes comes with an instructional DVD to ensure that the wearer has a successful brand experience while achieving the product's optimum benefits. While walking in the shoes, your core muscles are engaged and your body is in perfect alignment. Bringing significant physiological benefits to the serious walker, MBT is winning the brand race with no competitors in sight.

My friend Kym and I each dropped $250 for a pair–not inexpensive– but innovative brands do justify a premium price. The MBT trained salesman told us not to walk for more than fifteen minutes when wearing them for the first time. Kym and I readily agreed to his instructions, just before exchanging a mutually understood "yeah, right" glance, and setting out on a six-mile walk.

The curvature of the shoe gave us an unexpected spring in our steps, making us feel energetic and athletically invincible. But as we entered our last few miles, we realized that the man at the store wasn't kidding.

We practically crawled the last mile but gained a new respect for the brand and the workout we'd just endured. We were sore everywhere - inner thighs, back, butt, abs, and feet. Even while standing still in the shoes, these muscles were engaged. Our posture and gait improved, our muscles were firmer, and Kym now insists that MBT stands for "My Butt's Tighter."

CEO Conrad Casser explains the product's powerful point of differentiation. "We consider this a kinetic device. When you step on the soft heal sensor, it provides intentional instability and sends a signal to your brain, telling you to be more involved in the act of walking. This is basically the opposite of traditional footwear which is rigid and supportive and, in most cases, does the work that your feet and ankles normally do." Wearers also use three to four percent more oxygen while walking and report significant relief from lower back, neck and foot pain. The shoes are used by Olympic athletes and recommended by physical therapists.

In fact, MBT shoes are considered a medical device in Europe where they have been gaining popularity in the last ten years. They were introduced in the U.S. in 2003 when Casser acquired the distribution rights for North America. No paid advertising was used - word of mouth from end users, retailers and the media fueled their growth. "We're actually holding off customers now so we can keep a steady growth pattern," says Casser. And that's not easy to do when publicity from the *Today Show, Good Morning America*, and CNN is stepping up the pace of zealous consumers in their quest for the MBT.

Casser adds, "We achieved a sales level that was substantially higher than expected in the first year; in the second year we doubled that, and we're going to double again this year." While he doesn't expect that type of growth to endure forever, the company has already reached an important milestone, selling its one millionth pair worldwide in November of 2005. Shoes are now available through 500 U.S. retailers - primarily high end shoe stores - that must pass rigorous MBT standards before qualifying as a vendor – another smart move for brand consistency and success.

Ensuring that distributors can represent your product precisely as you intended is a crucial part of the brand continuum. MBT ensures success by qualifying their vendors and training them through their academy.

"We absolutely qualify our retailers and make sure they have the knowledge base to begin with," according to Rory Mitchell, National Sales and Marketing Director. "Our sales people are well educated – they have some type of medical background and are real experts. The academy ensures brand consistency worldwide."

With this type of success, imitators are bound to be afoot. But MBT is creating barriers to entry and imitation. "There are three patents on the product – heel sensor, rocker sole and pivot point," says Casser. The company leverages this proprietary difference through their point of purchase displays.

With first mover advantages, third party credibility through publicity, and a meticulous control of the distribution channel, this is a product that will be difficult to imitate - and if someone does, they will have to persuade millions of loyal followers to walk in another direction. Based on MBT's flawless attention to their brand, they're not likely to let that happen.

Brandstorming Questions

1. Is my company's research and development strong enough to create a product that renders others obsolete or outdated in:

   a. Packaging

   b. Design

   c. Delivery methods

   d. Environmental impact

2. How can I leverage this in my organization, positioning my brand as the only logical choice for consumers who want cutting edge concepts?

Strategy # 29:

Be true to your core beliefs

Rent.com - *www.rent.com*

"To me, branding is as much about action as it is about marketing," says Todd Katler of Rent.com. He joined the company as head of sales in June 2001, joining founders Scott Ingram and Alan Hunter. "Most people think that small and medium sized businesses are at a financial disadvantage and they can't serve the world, or are limited in what they can brand or not brand."

But being a small business didn't stop Rent.com from becoming a powerful online portal that successfully matched millions of renters with apartment communities. It didn't stop them from creating a positive brand experience for their clients. And in 2005, it didn't stop eBay from buying the company, according to Katler, for $433 million.

But it would take four years before Rent.com was ready for that acquisition. In its early days of operation, the struggling portal was not at all profitable. Katler recalls, "We needed to do the right thing in branding the company. We knew that we had two customers - renters looking for a new place to live, and property management companies trying to fill their vacancies. Every other company in our space focused solely on the property management companies because those are the people who write the checks. They did what the property managers asked them to do regardless of the validity of their request even if it wasn't in the best interests of the renter."

Rent.com had a different approach. Do what's best for the renter. They believed that if they did right by the end users, it would ultimately create more leases for the managers and both parties would have a successful brand experience.

The strategy worked. Katler says, "We made renters happier and in doing so, we created more and more leases and became the cornerstone product for our property management customers. We rapidly became the largest source of leases for many of them. We did it by listening to what renters wanted."

Choosing to focus on the needs of one primary market has inherent challenges–like turning away profitable opportunities that conflict with serving that market. Katler recalls, "It was hard because we had big property managers asking us to do something like put a huge banner ad on our site – this would alienate the renters. We could have charged a lot of money for the banner and gotten more clicks, but overall the renter experience would have been deteriorated."

To garner the attention of prospective renters, Rent.com employed pay-per-click advertising, affiliate partnerships and good search engine optimization. Katler says, "Our approach was to have as good a natural search placement as possible. The company name itself is clearly a winner – a name that renters would be likely to search for and remember." Rent.com also identified synergistic partners such as moving and utility companies that included Rent.com links on their sites.

Ninety percent of Rent.com's online inventory was built through a sales staff that conducted face to face and phone meetings with property managers. Today, the majority of the sales are accomplished telephonically without face to face interaction. This is in sharp contrast to the sales efforts of Rent.com competitors which accomplish nearly all their sales in person. Katler spoke of their sales approach. "That's never been done in our segment of the industry before at this scale," he says. "We took a leap of faith. You can't be afraid of making a mistake - it doesn't mean you should do things haphazardly. Have solid fundamentals and make decisions based on core principals or data and once you do that, it doesn't matter what happens, if it doesn't work fix it.

Nothing gets done without risk."

While Rent.com takes risks, it always keeps its eye on detailed metrics. It was successful at creating an online environment where everything could be tested down to the background of each page. And metrics, not consensus must prevail according to Katler. "If you get ten people in a room, you'll get ten different opinions. In the end, all we cared most about is what helped renters make the most leases. That solution that was best for business metrics was almost always the best solution."

He says that while everyone is entitled to their opinion, at some point you have to make objective decisions. And Rent.com's decision making has been solidly based in objective measurement of web analytics. He says, "We would run four or five of the same home pages and give an equal portion of the renter database to each version to test which one had the highest conversion. We just did some testing of many variants on our home page last month." Their system enables the company to evaluate consumer choices and make changes to maximize responses.

The combination of good metrics and making choices based on their core values and clients, simplifies decision making. Decisions are based on objective facts and on the basis of whether or not they support or negate the brand promise.

Katler says, "When you have a good working definition of who you are to your customers, you need to stay true to that." By staying true to the renters, they helped get more leases. Because they helped get more leases, they were able to charge property managers only when they were successful in making a match. "We were the only national source that they paid when they got a lease. There was no speculative advertising by our customers. It was all success based. Making our renters happy drives most of our business."

And Rent.com continues to find new ways to make renters happy, like launching complementary services to support its target audience. He says, "We keep growing through our typical core business." One product is "Gigamoves" (*www.gigamoves.com*) which connects renters with quality moving companies. Katler says, "Many of the solutions out there were disrespectful and poor experiences for both the renters and the moving companies. We launched the service to make the process better for renters. We have a screening process for moving companies and rigorous standards to get rid of companies who tell the renter it's going to cost $1000 and then bill for $2000. We've taken huge steps to create a better process – it's going great." Another product is a free service that connects roommates. By having a clear understanding of this primary market, Rent.com can continue to launch complementary products that support the core brand and create new income streams.

Another part of Rent.com's success in serving clients has been their ability to keep their autonomy after the acquisition. eBay kept every Rent.com staff member - ninety-seven in all. And Rent.com headquarters have remained in their Southern California home base while they reap the benefits and expertise of their parent company in the North. Katler says, "One of the biggest and most trusted brands with expertise in online transactions gave us wonderful assets." Despite being a part of one of the most well known brands in the world, Katler still keeps his perspective that size doesn't have to matter to be successful.

"Branding doesn't always mean Super Bowl commercials or logos on the side of a NASCAR – brand is what your customers think about. In our infancy stages we kept our brand central despite the business challenges, our brand was being experts at what we do; our brand was delivering a risk free solution; our brand was listening to our customers."

Brandstorming Questions

1. What are the core values that drive my organization?

2. Do these values guide my decision making to the extent that it creates a point of differentiation?

3. Do I ever compromise these values for a short term gain?

4. How can I leverage the organization to emphasize a values-based process that is in the best interest of my clients?

Strategy # 30:

Make an existing product better

Pure Pharmaceuticals, LLC - *www.sunpill.com*

Bob Bell has a tough act to follow – his own. As a college student in the eighties, he worked part time as a lifeguard on the shores of Miami Beach. At a young age, he was already in the business of protecting people from the water, but it was his ability to save people from the damaging rays of the sun that would give rise to a brand known to sun bathers everywhere.

Bell noticed that most beachgoers didn't like products available to them. He recalls, "At the time the only sun care products available were Coppertone and Hawaiian Tropic." He also observed that some people didn't use them at all and those that did often missed spots or didn't reapply frequently enough. None of the products offered significant protection from the sun. These observations would later pay off for the budding entrepreneur.

There are now more than 1.3 million new cases of skin cancer diagnosed annually. "The incidence of melanoma has nearly tripled in the last four decades - a rate faster than that of any other cancer." Exposure to the sun's ultraviolet (UV) rays plays a major contributing role. And while practicing good habits – like using sun screen, can help prevent the disease, most Americans do not consistently protect themselves from the sun. The Centers for Disease Control and Prevention report that nearly 43 percent of white children under age twelve had at least one sunburn during the past year. Bell knew that the sun had damaging effects even in the eighties before it was a newsworthy item. He decided to write his college marketing thesis on promoting a sun care product that had three points of differentiation over the current market's major brands.

"The people that I used to see while working on the beach just wanted to get a tan. Coppertone and Hawaiian Tropic were greasy – people didn't like putting them on and had a hard time getting them off when they took a shower. I also knew that skin cancer was growing so I based the product line on having protective qualities. Finally I knew that the packaging could be improved to differentiate against existing products."

Bell worked on designing a product that was ultra lightweight, not greasy. He also focused on sun protection. Finally, he designed different packaging. The leading brands were in brown bottles. Bell says, "I made my packages colorful and bright – some packaging was in clear bottles so you could see the product. The design made the bottles pop off the shelf." Bob not only looked different from his competitors; he was different. In addition to having three strong points of differentiation, he leveraged the fact that his competitors were multibillion dollar drug companies. "I took advantage of being small and introduced new ideas and product technology to market more quickly." He ultimately launched the product that was the subject of his college paper. He called it Banana Boat.

"I started the product from zero and built it into the second largest brand," Bell recalls. Fifteen years later, Bell and a private equity partner sold Banana Boat to Playtex for a reported $90 million.

So how do you top that? Staying within the industry he knew, Bell decided to improve upon the very product he himself helped create. His next bright idea was SunPill.

The once a day tablet is designed to work in conjunction with sunscreen by supporting the body's natural defenses against the sun. "Sun damage occurs at the cellular level," Bell explains, "and there's no product that addresses that issue. Sunscreen protects you from the top layer only, and none are 100 percent effective."

Unfortunately, years of misleading information on sun care product effectiveness have many consumers burning up. A current class action law suit filed in the state of California is now claiming fraud, negligence and intentional deception due to the use of terms like "waterproof," "all-day protection," and "sun block" against brands like Coppertone, Hawaiian Tropic, Bull Frog and Neutrogena and even Banana Boat.

"There's no such thing as sunblock," says Bell, "Nothing can block 100 percent of the rays. Even though the FDA established guidelines in 1999 which banned claims like 'all day,' 'waterproof,' and 'sunblock' on sunscreen labels, which may be unsupported and potentially misleading, they delayed their own guidelines to allow the industry time to do more research." In other words, FDA compliance in this area is currently voluntary. Bell says, "Sunscreens also block UVB rays but have little effect on UVA rays which cause cancer. And even those who use it don't reapply often enough or they'll miss spots. Sunpill is an extra layer of protection – it works from the inside out."

Bell is working with scientists and doctors on the product. He is using natural ingredients that have protective properties including nutrients, herbs, vitamins, and antioxidants. "We launched this product about six months ago at the American Academy of Dermatologists which is the largest dermatological organization in the world. It was well received but it's interesting because they initially didn't understand it – they weren't taught about this in medical school – it's a new innovation. They didn't understand how the product worked but once they saw the studies and the science, they liked it."

Bell's challenge in marketing is that he is creating a new category in the marketplace. Buyers don't have a frame of reference on how this product compares to others. To give buyers a point of parity and difference to other sun products, Bell gave the product a name that would be easy to understand. "It would cost a fortune to give the public awareness through advertising," says Bell. "I chose the name so that consumers could easily understand what the product is."

Will competitors soon follow with SunPill rivals? Bell isn't worried. "Mainly the sunscreen companies are drug or consumer product companies and sunscreen sales are a small part of their business. We're cultivating the dermatologist community and explaining what it is and trying to get them to recommend the product to their patients."

Bell has also hired a medium-sized PR agency to leverage the unique offering. "The PR in just the last couple months totaled over 50 million gross impressions. (Gross impressions refers to number of exposures your target market has to your message.) We've been on shows like *Good Morning America*, *World News Tonight*, MSNBC, and magazines like *Redbook*, and *Cosmopolitan*. We did it through PR because the product is so different."

While some skin care professionals find the Sunpill concept hard to swallow, many of them have based their criticism on the use of the pill by itself – which is not Bell's recommendation. The pill is designed as an add-on product to sunscreen. Perry Robbins, M.D. president and founder of the Skin Cancer Foundation and supporter of SunPill, agrees, "By blending antioxidants, vitamins and plant extracts that work at your skin's cellular level, sun pills help support your natural defenses against the sun but they don't provide enough protection on their own, so combine them with a topical sunscreen."

With endorsements from the medical community and through public relations efforts, the product is rapidly gaining third party credibility. Bell says, "My initial plan is to build some traction because the product is only available now through website and through some dermatologists' offices. Next year we will launch it into retail stores."

It's hard to make revenue projections on sales of the pill which currently retails for about $1 a day. There is no historical data to use as a guideline, but Bell is optimistic about the medical community's warm reception and the product research. "The company just got test reports that indicate the product is very effective." Some of the tests show extraordinary results, but unfortunately, due to FDA guidelines they cannot be publicly announced in product marketing for the over the counter product. Bell explains, "Regulations restrict what you can say in this category." The report will be published and given to the doctors. "The word will get around," he says.

"I think branding is built on reputation and quality and I think sometimes it's perception as much as substance; but for a product like this, you have to have substance." Endorsements from the medical community backed by empirical data are designed to do just that. While it is still too early to determine the success of the new product, Bell's track record combined with a strongly differentiated product could result in a bright forecast for the entrepreneur who, after all these years, is still in the business of saving lives.

Brandstorming Questions

1. Does my product or offering enhance existing products in the market?

2. How can I leverage synergies that exist with my product and another existing product or service?

3. If my product is one of a kind, am I using PR to generate no-cost media coverage?

Strategy # 31:

Marry branding with direct response

Ben Mack

www.thinktwoproductsahead.com

David Garfinkel

www.worldcopyrightinginstitute.com

When it comes to marketing executives and sales executives, can't we all just get along? The widely known tension that exists between sales and marketing has long and tangled roots that can be traced to the bipolar orientations of each. The goal of sales is to close a deal today. The goal of marketing is to close a deal tomorrow, and the next month and the next year.

So, if marketing and sales have a hard time coexisting, it's not surprising that the same is true for branding and direct marketing – they share a similar plight. Branding says, "Our products will elevate your body, mind and spirit." Direct marketing says, "Order now and we'll throw in a free Ginsu knife." You can see how the two might just grate on each other's nerves.

Before the 1990's, the disconnection could be easily spotted. Ben Mack, author of *Think Two Products Ahead* (Wiley 2007) recalls, "An automotive company would run an elegant branding ad about their vehicle on a national level. But local ads for the dealership would use any tone, look, or message to drive people onto the showroom floor. Local ads would say anything to incite immediate action and they didn't necessarily help the overall image of the company." But he remembers when all of that changed. "I think Mitsubishi cracked the code to merge branding and sales. Their national campaign used a theme of 'Wake Up and Drive.' The direct mail campaign used the same tagline and generated traffic into the showrooms while still keeping the consistency of the brand look and message."

When Mack met current partner David Garfinkel – a direct marketing expert and established copywriter (*www.world-copywriting-institute.com*), it could have been an unlikely partnership. But the two have shown that branding and direct marketing can not only coexist – but share wedded bliss - and their clients are living happily ever after with campaigns that offer the immediacy of direct mail and the long term benefits of powerful branding.

Mack says of the marriage of the two concepts, "We believe this is rare and new. With most direct marketing people, you mention branding and they snort. Their eyes roll heavenward. Most branding types will avoid the issue of sales." It wouldn't have been surprising if either of them had cold feet prior to their business partnership. They both witnessed the excessive anal retentiveness of branders who are often perfectionists to the point of absurdity.

Garfinkel's opinion of branding was marred by an experience he had when a friend of his relayed a story of an audio/video production he was doing for an ad agency. The agency wanted to use the same musical note of "C" that was used in the Honda commercials. For those of you who aren't trained in music, there is only one "C". If you change it to a slightly higher or lower pitch, it's no longer a "C". Honda doesn't own the rights to a special "C", yet the fact that someone was certain they did is typical of similar scenarios that leave direct marketers with a bad taste in their mouth about all branding types.

It's not that Garfinkel is opposed to consistency – just foolish consistency. He says, "The essence of brand is about a consistency of the customer's feeling, impression, relationship, and opinion toward the company. Even Ralph Waldo Emerson said, 'Foolish consistency is the hobgoblin of small minds.'"

Mack had a similar experience while a Senior VP of Strategy at worldwide advertising giant BBDO, working on a Cingular account which had an advertising budget of $60 billion – for one month. Mack witnessed a branding executive who almost held up 40 million FSI's (free standing inserts) which are inserted into newspapers. The inserts were to announce Cingular's Rollover Minutes campaign, a pricing plan that allowed unused minutes from one month to roll over into subsequent months. The ad exec nearly brought the inserts to a halt because he felt they didn't have the right shade of orange.

It's no wonder Mack proclaims, "Branding is an extended seduction, not a color palette." He also simplifies the frequently misunderstood term of "branding" to a simple concept. He says, "I suggest you think of the word "brand" as the likelihood a customer will do business with you *again*." Now that's a practical concept that just about any direct marketer can get behind.

Mack and Garfinkel's disdain for those mired in marketing minutia, facilitated a common bond that has enabled them to merge two seemingly opposing but powerful forces of marketing. Garfinkel says, "When I met Ben, I understood what he had to say about stories, relationships, and reputation. It actually overlaps with some of the things that I work on in direct marketing copy. It's just common sense – it's what works for companies who are very successful in their relationship with their customers."

So how do you merge branding with direct marketing? Mack and Garfinkel have found a way. When you understand the simplicity and the brilliance of their process, you'll wonder – why did it take so long for someone to figure this out?

Garfinkel talks about what sells in direct marketing. "Direct response is much more about the now – it's about how am I going to affect my life today – how is this going to deliver the emotional fulfillment that I'm looking for in a very short period of time?" He outlines the seven drivers of direct response marketing:

1. **Make money**

2. **Save money**

3. **Save time**

4. **Save effort**

5. **Avoid pain**

6. **Improve health**

7. **Move towards pleasure**

It's hard to disagree that these are powerful motivators but how do you fit them in with branding's messages which are often more subtle and complex? Mack has a three-step process of building a brand. He suggests that all ad agencies do the same thing: synthesize, extract, and amplify their brand essence.

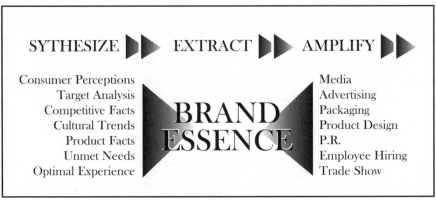

Mack's three-step approach to brand building.

But what is your brand essence? Mack defines brand essence as the mental territory where you have an advantage. It's the reason customers give you money. He uses examples of Corona – their brand essence isn't about the flavor of the beer – it's about playtime.

You can probably think of other examples where you've paid for the brand and not the product itself. You didn't buy Domino's pizza because it's the best tasting pizza in town – you bought it because you wanted to eat in thirty minutes or less.

Why do people pay for your services? It may not be the obvious answer that you think it is. Once you can define it, you can amplify it in many ways – one being direct marketing. Mack and Garfinkel spoke about a case study in which they beautifully merged these two concepts for a company which had commodity written all over it.

Financial planning – it's one of those "everybody looks alike and does the same thing" categories, right? Their client was able to grow a respectable business but needed to take it to the next level.

The client sold a $2,000 home study course on investing to build wealth and had 500 satisfied subscribers. The biggest qualm from their prospects, Fundamentalist Christians, was that it was viewed as gambling. Garfinkel recalls, "We had morally based people saying this product is working. We wanted to take it to the masses – build it through word of mouth. We looked at the concept of brand essence –in this case, 'responsibility fulfilled.' In other words, if you make wise investment choices, you are being responsible and fulfilling that responsibility." This was a concept that would be more acceptable to this conservative audience. He adds, "Then we took it down to a more ground level experience or ground level expression. We went through the seven drivers and narrowed it down to 'make money.'" But they had to communicate this in a way that would be receptive to this special group.

Garfinkel states, "Ideas spread quickly through closed communities which offer word of mouth and trust. So if one person says it is working, others will believe it but if you take it to the masses, it can look like a sleazy infomercial as opposed to a product that helps people."

Garfinkel drilled down to how the business came to be. The founder of the company believed that religion comes first, then family and then nation. He wasn't just getting wealthy on his own – he felt he had a moral responsibility to share it to help others fulfill their responsibilities to the church and their family. The concept was different from everything else. The brand essence— "responsibility fulfilled"—would appeal to a larger audience; anyone with a family realizes they have responsibilities to their families. Even people that don't have families have a sense of responsibility to themselves or others. Additional money is going to help you meet that.

But the brand essence—taking responsibility—is a conflict of direct marketing which says "Take action now." Garfinkel states, "Because direct response is much more about the now, how could we convey this? We looked at how one would be making money quickly with a higher degree of security rather than with gambling and how this would work in terms of responsibility fulfilled. Our headline read, 'Have you found that your six figure income isn't giving you everything you thought you would get?'."

Garfinkel states, "We started developing specific scenarios about how people were going to get $20-30K for their kids' private schools if they're living month to month on $100K per year. We developed specific sales points around this. If people were to make more money, then they wouldn't have the time for their family and wouldn't be able to contribute to their community—a no win situation."

But this program enabled people to build wealth with a system that required a ninety minute investment per week. They could be greatly increasing income and cash on hand. "This means that by wisely investing, they would do both, short term gain and long term goals; a successful marriage of two opposing concepts." And that's how the marriage of branding and direct marketing works.

Mack also demonstrated the merger of the two concepts when he worked at J. Walter Thompson. There he won the 1998 Silver Effie award from the American Marketing Association for his work on Yomega Yo-Yo's taking it from $8 to $120 million in one year. Mack recalls, "Most toy ads were based around the idea of 'simply buy this now and have this type of experience.'"

With the Yomega Yo-Yo account, Mack focused on making the product a form of self expression. Suddenly, the brand essence was not about the yo-yo, but about the notion of mastering the yo-yo. "We had teams of yo-yo experts going out to different schools and teaching yo-yoing. There was a two fold message. You need to buy the yo-yo (direct response) and you want to experience a greater mastery of yo-yoing, which is self expression (branding). There was explosive growth by marrying branding with direct marketing," says Mack.

Mack concludes "It's not a matter of making the immediate sale; it's about making the next sale. The highest cost we have as marketers is getting the initial customer. Once you have the customer it's about the ongoing relationship." Garfinkel adds, "The invitation for the large opportunity is built into the short term."

The two have successfully married two powerful marketing concepts. When a company can achieve that, it will be perhaps the most important merger in the history of their business.

Brandstorming Questions

1. Is my brand conveyed in my advertising or is there a disconnection between the brand message and a strong call to action advertising message? For example, a Harvard trained plastic surgeon whose surgeries range from $5,000 to $20,000 is situated in an elegantly designed Beverly Hills office. His ads make him look like a big discounter with headlines that read "One Free Liposuction with Facelift!" These ads may generate calls, but do not convey the high end nature of the brand or the quality of services provided creating a mixed message in the mind of the consumer.

2. What am I doing to ensure that my brand and my marketing are merged with consistent imagery and messaging?

Strategy # 32:

Be a control freak

CAM Commerce Solutions, Inc. - *www.camcommerce.com*

Geoff Knapp wasn't about to let someone else sell his product. "If you let dealers work with your customers, then they have the relationship." And the man who brought CAM Commerce from inception to a $26 million publicly traded company with 10,000 customers, ought to know what's best.

A lot of companies offer the same services as CAM; inventory management, POS Software, and accounting systems for retailers and etailers. But CAM's competitors sold their products through dealers to help them quickly build their business. Knapp took a different approach. He realized that the value of his business was not in the offering but in building a customer base. Those instincts would later pay off in a big way.

"Our reach wasn't as good at first. At one time, we only had about fifteen locations around the country. Our competition has more locations but had a smaller part of each sale that they had to split with their dealers."

At some point, when selling technology products, you will get to a place where everyone is making the same claims for the same products to the same list of prospects. To make things more difficult, marketing to retailers and etailers means you have to create a value proposition to appeal to a wide array of vertical markets, each with their own specific needs. You have to understand and address the nuances of each business.

"The retailer has a lot of sophisticated, vastly different needs," says Knapp. "They don't want to pay a lot but they want a lot of help. You can't market to them the same way. You can't brand yourself to a liquor store and a health food store in the same way."

CAM gained new customers by focusing in some specific vertical markets and offering one source solutions like Retail ICE which became the number one retail system. They enabled their clients to work with one reliable vendor who could help them grow through training, customer support, and access to additional products they would need along the way.

At one time, CAM gave the Retail ICE system away for free (a retail value of $3995). By getting prospects engaged through the free product, CAM was able to deliver a brand experience of customer services while introducing clients to new solutions they would need to grow their business.

CAM continues to deliver on their brand promise of a one-source solution and top notch customer services by having forty full time dedicated customer service technicians available twenty-four hours a day through a toll-free number. Customers receive real-time support to keep their system and their businesses running smoothly. CAM also offers two advanced training facilities to guarantee that customers will learn how to use the product successfully.

CAM also helped make their customers successful by building features into to the software that would increase sales: customer loyalty reward features, gift card support, traditional mail and e-mail marketing, buyer behavior tracking, customer database with service tracking, and an internet store for e-commerce. Their customer base grew as retailers responded to the ease of the one source solution and the support that was offered. Most retailers are not technologically savvy; they just need to know enough about the product to run their business. CAM made that possible.

Today CAM's clients range from small and medium sized companies to national brands like New Balance, the Cincinnati Bengals, Universal Studios and the New York Yankees. And by keeping his customers happy—and close—Knapp was able to act on a technology that would bring a significant and less challenging source of revenue to the company that would work the same in any vertical market: payment processing. CAM provides the software to allow the integration of the payment processing system for free in order to get the processing business.

The system can work in any vertical says Knapp, "We don't make money on the razors blades, we make it on the razors." The razors refers to the swipe of the credit card through the system: with each swipe, dollars are generated to CAM's bottom line. Best of all, the system works in any vertical market—tire stores, dental offices, restaurants—so there's no costs associated with modifying the product to a particular vertical.

"We were well positioned to take this technology on because we control the whole channel and have a connection with the customer; we have a sustainable value that way," says Knapp. He continues, "Because we already have a lot of customers, it motivated us to try harder and to look for more ways to do things and monetize our customer base. The credit card piece really worked for us. It represents about $12 million a year and is growing at $4 million a year. Half of the revenue drops to the bottom line." CAM's sales are expected to exceed $30 million over the next twelve months.

By keeping his eye on his customers, Knapp was positioned to find a new revenue stream that offsets the more complex, customized solutions of CAM's original offering. It's enough to keep both customers and shareholders happy.

CAM was recently named in "Fortune's Top 100 Small Businesses" for America's fastest growing small companies. It's not surprising that CAM would get the attention of *Forbes*. They offer everything *Forbes* looks for in a small business: a quality product, outstanding customer service, and a healthy bottom line to shareholders. Of course, a little control couldn't hurt.

Brandstorming Questions

1. Am I focusing on too many markets rather than focusing on a few vertical markets where I can make the biggest impact?

2. Does my system ensure that I, rather than my distributors, have access to the end users of the product?

3. Can I and should I provide a one-source solution for my services? What are the benefits or disadvantages of doing so?

Strategy # 33:

Take care of your employees and they will take care of the brand

Pret a Manger - *www.Pret.com*

Pret A Manger receives 70,000 inquiries a year from people who want to work for their company – only 6 percent will ever make it to an interview. Pret doesn't sell luxury sports cars, high end couture or cutting edge technology. They sell sandwiches.

The wildly successful, often irreverent culinary gem of London has created a brand that is growing in the hearts and mouths of patrons who enjoy Pret's no-nonsense approach and their high quality "fast" food. The name is from the French phrase prêt à manger (pronounced Pret uh mahn ZHAY), meaning "ready to eat."

The company was founded in 1986 when friends, Sinclair Beecham and Julian Metcalfe, who shared a passion for food, longed for a place that used natural ingredients with no chemicals or additives. They couldn't find such a place so they created their own.

Each of Pret's 150 shops has its own kitchen where sandwiches are made on the day of purchase. Unsold products are given to the homeless. Pret uses cardboard containers for their fresh sandwiches instead of plastic boxes which would suggest that they can be kept over night. Also on the menu are filled baguettes, soup, salads, desserts, muffins, cakes, croissants, all made with no additives or preservatives. The fresh approach has been well received by patrons and Pret is now in its twentieth year of doing things in their own special way.

And their way is a far cry from traditional marketing and business methods. Commercial Director Simon Hargraves says, "We're quite a maverick in a way. To be honest, we don't hold focus groups; we don't buy research; we don't do anything normal. We try to cut out all the corporateness that can develop: no press team, no graphic design team, no strategy team, and no brand book. It's sometimes difficult for people to join us if they're used to having a brand book."

But it doesn't seem to deter those who are applying in droves to the company that only accepts one out of fourteen applicants. There are simply not enough positions available to accept more. Why the attraction to working at Pret? "We pay well above minimum wage," says Hargraves. Employees also qualify for a mystery shopper bonus. That's a bonus of £1.50 (about $2.86 US dollars) times forty hours of their workweek, if a mystery shopper comes into the shop and has a satisfactory experience. Pret also has staff parties, nights out, and free food which amount to the equivalent of about $50 US dollars a week. Pret also focuses heavily on training including programs that develop team building, time management, and coaching skills.

The bottom line is, Pret takes care of employees and happy employees take care of the brand. Libby Sartain, co-author of *Brand from the Inside* (Jossey-Bass, 2006) states that an employer's brand can emotionally connect employees so that they in turn deliver what the company promises to customers. Pret's promise and passion of quality food, high nutrition, and a fun environment has been consistently delivered by their staff. And that's a good thing for a company that only has three people on their marketing team. Much is accomplished through the customer experience and the word of mouth that follows.

According to Hargraves, "a lot of our marketing is done in store." He also says, "We have a particular look with pictures of food." The pictures position the food in unique ways, and convey the humor of the brand, like a piece of bread cut out to look like a car, or vegetables positioned to resemble a smiley face. The humor of the Pret brand is carried through in the employee-customer interaction.

"The promotional copy in Pret's published materials emulates the style of founder Julian Metcalfe who has a very direct way of talking," says Hargraves. He describes the tone as "cheeky." This can be seen in a brochure that says, "Low fat chocolate cake is stupid." "It's harsh and funny in some ways," says Hargraves. "We're renowned for that."

And the word– cheeky or not – is spreading. "Although we don't have a PR team, we get six or seven PR inquires each week. We don't do advertising, but we have window posters. Our marketing budget is very small, but we have a cult following."

The simplicity of their approach is also applied to making decisions about product offerings, Hargraves says. Team members sit around a table and talk about which new menu items should be included. "It's about what we like. What has worked for Pret is to go with our own convictions - a passion for food and the market we're in." Pret regularly keeps in touch with customers through letters, the company website, and calls in to Pret managers. "They're quite happy to tell us when things are going good or bad," says Hargraves. And Pret listens.

The consistency and culture has been self perpetuating. Founder Julian Metcalfe is still with the company. Hargraves says, "As you build the culture up in the company, people protect it naturally. It seems to work." This retailer significantly invests in recruiting, training, and compensating talent which has been essential to the company's success. After an interview, the candidate has an opportunity to work in a Pret shop. The shop team then votes on the candidate's ability to cut the mustard, or in this case, the baguette. The lucky few who are selected, enter a ten-day training program which ensures consistency of service and a positive brand experience for their customers.

Pret also empowers employees to use their best judgment to keep customers happy. An employee might offer a free beverage to a customer who's had to wait too long. And they are eager to stay with the company that trains, rewards, and empowers them. Pret's turnover rate is a low 4 percent. Hargraves, who has been with the company for nine years says, "We have people with the company for ten years and five people with fifteen years of service." Eighty percent of those who started with the company have been promoted to management positions. The biggest challenge in keeping people is that there are only so many positions available. "If you're in a specialist position it's difficult to move around," he says.

But that may not be the case for long. The company will be adding seven more shops in Hong Kong by the end of 2006. Once a franchise model, the company has brought all but five franchises back into the fray, which is often helpful in consistency of brand execution.

Pret launches new products every month to keep the range varied and exciting. Hargraves says, "We have standard and temporary menu items. If we change something, we'll get letters because we've taken out the pecan pie or a particular baguette." Their customers feel very comfortable making their feelings known and that's to be expected from a company that is big on communication.

Any of Pret's 3000 team members could talk to any of Pret's six directors at any time. "Some of our marketing copy gives the number of Metcalfe's office," Hargraves says. "A customer can go to Julian directly. It does make a difference."

"We have 400 to 500 customer contacts each week," says Hargraves. "They email us through our website, use a comment card in our shops, or make comments to managers who log the information on to the company system or help desk."

The system has made Pret a winner with their patrons. The company has recently ranked second only to Google as a preferred brand in the UK's Voltage 100 Poll. In 2002, *Fortune* magazine named the company one of the "10 Best Companies to Work In" in Europe. With all the attention, it would seem logical that imitators of the brand would follow, but what's surprising is how imitators are getting Pret's recipes.

Pret publishes their recipes which are widely available for public viewing. Hargraves adds, "We wanted customers to understand that our products are something they could make at home if they had time to do it. Our ingredients are the same as what you'd have in your own cupboard –from the fridge – not from a factory or processing plant."

But Pret's team is fully aware that it takes more than a recipe to capture their special brand of magic, much of which is in their execution. "We have quite a huge number of private companies who try to do it in foreign countries where we're not present. We have a case now in Spain by someone who has copied the recipes. Someone in Russia copied our store look, but it was appallingly executed."

Despite the copycats, Pret's not afraid of a little competition. "There is a mutual respect for our competitors," says Hargraves. "I know they're in our shops each week and there is some copying going on occasionally, but that's quite healthy." But he adds, "If someone copies them, they would fail to have their own personality." And Pret is all about personality.

Hargraves says, "People see us as a vibrant brand with huge potential." And that includes some very important people. In 2001, McDonald's bought a 33 percent non-controlling stake in the company. He adds, "McDonald's has a separate arm called McDonald's Ventures. They've invested in many partner brands around the world. It has helped them to understand a bit more about other markets."

The partnership has enabled Pret to tap into the purchasing power of the industry giant without changing the company's autonomy, brand or methods. Hargraves says, "They had the skills we needed to move into Hong Kong and New York." Despite some customers who called it a "sellout," Pret sales went up dramatically and quickly following McDonald's presence. "Whenever there is a take over, there is a backlash," he says. "But nothing really changed. We're still privately owned by six people including McDonald's. But McDonald's doesn't have any rights in the company. It's been a good deal for both of us."

It certainly hasn't stopped Pret from continuing their tradition of creating quality food and happy employees. They've known instinctively what some companies have yet to learn: employees are the face of the company and can make or break the brand experience.

The company has clearly found a recipe for building a strong brand by taking care of the people who take care of their customers. And their numbers reflect the growth that comes with a great customer experience. Pret's net income in 2004 was $12.8 million, a 733 percent increase over the previous year.

Despite their success, the company has been able to keep perspective, and while they're rigorous about providing quality food and customer service, they don't take themselves too seriously. Hargraves jokes, "At the end of the day, we're not saving the world – we're only selling lunch."

Brandstorming Questions

1. Does my brand attract employees? What elements would be needed to ensure that I had more applicants than positions available – to enable me to select the best and the brightest?

2. What aspects of my company could be improved to attract employees?

   a. Work environment?

   b. Culture?

   c. Pay?

   d. Training programs?

   e. Other?

3. How can I translate happy employees into a better brand experience for my customers?

   a. Empowering employees to do whatever it takes to make customers happy?

   b. Letting employees use a certain type of language or style to communicate my brand with customers? (i.e., joking, conversational, shocking, sarcastic, reserved, sophisticated?)

4. How can I use imagery in the presence of the customer that conveys the brand personality?

    a. Posters

    b. Signs

    c. Menus, handouts, brochures

    d. Design of my offices

    e. Appearance of employees, uniforms

    f. Other

Strategy # 34:

Mass customize

Laptop Design USA - *www.laptopdesignusa.com*

What if you had a laptop computer that was so cool, no one would steal it? It sounds like an oxymoron – but then again, so does the term "mass customization."

Peder Blohm is the founder of Laptop Design USA, a company that will create a professional quality customized graphic of your choosing on your laptop which will not only look great – it will serve as a theft deterrent. The distinctive look will make it more conspicuous and therefore, less desirable to thieves, who want to quickly unload their stash. And with laptop theft reaching reported estimates of nearly one million units annually, what laptop owner wouldn't at least give this concept some serious consideration?

Mass customization gives customers an opportunity to have a customized experience while still benefiting from the high volume discounts associated with mass production. In today's instant gratification market, companies who can mass customize will have a captive audience. Laptop Design USA's process also brings the customer into the design process and in doing so is able to track data on consumer preferences with each order taken. The process of involving the customer in product design was described in Alvin Toffler's *Future Shock* (Bantam Books, 1970) which referred to this type of customer as a "prosumer" – a producer as well as a consumer who can define and produce the product.

In operation for less than a year, Laptop Design USA has a concept that is taking off with individuals and companies nationwide. Blohm, the consummate entrepreneur and brand specialist who was responsible for introducing drag racing and American muscle cars to Sweden, can't help but recognize a great concept when he sees one.

While watching an episode of *Fox and Friends,* he noticed three people conversing on a couch. On the coffee table in front of them were two laptop computers with open lids. "I was watching the program while working out of my home and saw the laptops. One had a Fox News sticker slapped on it – I said, 'one can do better than that.'"

Blohm immediately went to work researching the market. He first asked himself, "Is someone already doing this?" They weren't. "Is there a market out there for this?" There was. In 2005, 16.2 million laptops were sold in the U.S. "The market was as big as new car sales," Blohm says. Blohm started doing patent research and did all his homework about production methods, logistics and other relevant issues. He looked into the mechanics of how they would transform the customized laptop lid without disrupting the function of the computer.

The company was launched in September 2005. Cover designs ranged from logos to puppies, limited only by the imaginations of the prosumers. The idea caught on quickly. As Blohm points out, "We're now doing a program for a leading manufacturer of sports shoes and sneakers. They have more than 170 agents nationwide."

So how *do* you wrench 170 laptops out of the clenched fists of a busy sales team? Very carefully, of course. But Blohm has the situation covered. His company will send a specially designed DHL box to the laptop owner in the afternoon; Laptop Design USA will receive the laptop the next morning. Blohm says, "You put your computer in the box and off it goes. We have pre-made lids from the manufactures with the new design already applied. We put the new lid on and the laptop goes back out to you the next morning—with turnaround times that can be as quick as one day." The design process involves replacing the lids only; it will not interfere with the internal mechanisms of the computer or impact its warranty. That's enough to ease the fears of even the most anxious laptop owners.

Of course, something this big is bound to attract imitators, right? Blohm has already addressed this issue, "If you look at the computer industry, you'll see that there are basically five original design manufactures (ODM's) and they're all in China and Malaysia. They are producing 90 percent of all of the laptops for IBM/Lenovo, Gateway, Dell, Toshiba, Acer, HP and others."

"Gateway and others don't want to get into performing any additional services," according to Blohm. "Manufacturers in China could do it for them, but would require a minimum order of 250,000 units. They prefer to outsource customization and personalization."

Blohm believes that laptops have become a commodity. "What happens now is the laptops are losing any competitive edge because every laptop has the same guts in them. The only thing they can compete with is speed, memory, weight, battery life. Now by using our service, they're getting something that I call a sellable difference."

Laptop Design USA VP of Sales Andy Pais, says that when it comes to laptops, "personalization and fashion are the next big thing in laptops. Our company even makes matching laptop cases bearing the same design as the computer inside."

Blohm works with any size business or any individual. He says, "We market to large corporations like an insurance company that purchases 16,000 units per year, with a duck sitting on it. We work with companies or individuals. The market is so big, there's room for everybody."

And everybody includes schools and universities who have become interested in the antitheft component of the system. Blohm says, "Ninety-five percent of laptop theft is on impulse. The customized graphic makes the thief move on to the next opportunity." He adds, "Prices vary depending on the type of computer and complexity of design; it can be compared to a couple of business lunches. It is not a bad investment to save a computer from the hands of a thief and be fashionable at the same time."

The added brand benefit to companies is to have thousands of sales reps sporting their logos around the country or the world.

The designs will become walking billboards and you can already imagine how companies will find clever ways to exploit the new medium.

Tell others about your brand without saying a word.

The company is marketing to individual buyers through a clever website which displays product designs and has contests like, "Pimp the Laptop" where viewers can compete and vote for their favorite design. Some contest entries included a record player turntable design, a butterfly, and an American flag. Viewers can also design a laptop online choosing from sample colors and logos. It's an interactive experience that will certainly appeal to the younger market.

The company has relied on public relations strategies to generate tens of thousands of page views to the site each month. But whether it's businesses or individuals who are using the products, the design factor is creating a buzz. One realtor who put her tagline on her laptop ended up getting two new clients while sitting at a local coffee shop and displaying her newly customized laptop. Another business executive believes the design just adds to the high end image of his company. Whether fashion or function is the motivator, the product will give each user a personalized brand experience and a little positive publicity. And that's hard to top.

Brandstorming Questions

1. Are there opportunities for mass customization in my company?

2. If I can't use mass customization per se, what things can I do to create a more personalized and memorable experience with each and every customer and prospect?

Strategy # 35:

Change the world

Perverted Justice - *www.perverted-justice.com*

If brands can change our behaviors, then brands can change our world. The last of our thirty-five strategies comes from what is arguably the most important brand of our time, because its mission is to protect our world's most precious resources—our children—from evil.

There is nothing more gut-wrenching than the subject of child molestation. Our minds can barely grasp its existence much less its pervasiveness. Thankfully, for all of us, one unassuming man—a self-proclaimed "computer geek" —decided to engage in a battle with an invisible and ubiquitous enemy in what could become the David & Goliath epic of our century.

Xavier Von Erck, the founder of Perverted Justice, was a frequent visitor to regional chat rooms in his home state of Oregon. He was stunned by how openly and unabashedly adult men solicited minors online. Von Erck recalls, "You'd see guys come into the chat rooms and, in the open area where everyone could see, try to get people that everyone knew was underage, to talk to them privately." And with that recognition, the plan to capture a predator was set in motion.

Von Erck logged onto a chat room, posing as a minor. As he expected, within seconds, sexual solicitations from adult men came forth. He then began doing something that was not being done on any other website: posting full, unedited conversations between predator and would-be prey; conversations like this one between a school teacher and someone he thought was an underage girl:

WBSooner (10:14:50 PM): we didnt get to talk the other day

FancyDancer14 (10:15:00 PM): mom was coming

FancyDancer14 (10:15:03 PM): lol

FancyDancer14 (10:15:17 PM): scared crap out of me lol

WBSooner (10:15:30 PM): does she not like you on there

FancyDancer14 (10:15:50 PM): dont like me talkin to peple I dont know

FancyDancer14 (10:16:18 PM): have to be careful

WBSooner (10:17:08 PM): yeah

WBSooner (10:17:13 PM): so how have you been

FancyDancer14 (10:17:29 PM): pretty gud i gues. hate skool

WBSooner (10:17:35 PM): she especially wouldnt like me

FancyDancer14 (10:17:40 PM): y

WBSooner (10:17:51 PM): cause I am gonna f- - - her little girl

(source: www.perverted-justice.com)

"School teachers represent more predators than any other occupation we see," says Von Erck, "but we find men from all occupations soliciting minors online," including a rabbi, a member of the department of homeland security, musicians, business owners, and the list goes on. Men make up about 95 percent of the predators seen by Perverted Justice and Von Erck believes this is a representative sample of predators as a whole. The web conversation listed above is less graphic than most, which often include photographs of the predator's genitals or vivid descriptions of sexual acts.

Von Erck has been as smart about his branding as he is at catching predators. He knew that he had to prove himself before getting police support, and created a meticulous process to ensure he would catch the right people.

"You have to get the first conviction before anyone will listen to you," he said. "We did a sting with media in Michigan, staged at a residential location." One of the predators who was captured at the house was so upset he actually complained to the police about being the victim of a sting while in pursuit of a minor. The police arrested him. Von Erck's testimony supported the evidence and the predator became the first of scores of convictions facilitated by Perverted Justice to date.

Von Erck's relationship with the media didn't end in Michigan. Programs around the country including *Court TV*, the *CBS Evening News*, and NBC's *Dateline* have captured the Perverted Justice process online and the once grassroots organization with ten volunteers now has thousands – all of whom undergo significant background checks designed to keep predators out. Von Erck's knack for this program also includes steering clear of associations with political or religious groups. "We have atheists working alongside Catholics," according to Von Erck. "We're a secular organization and aren't motivated by religious or political agendas."

His attention to detail ensures that the right people will be caught and convicted; he has volunteers who meticulously create profiles of the fictitious minors to make them look real. Von Erck states, "We are actually marketing something that looks like a kid."

He describes one of the more disturbing transactions of a man who brought his five-year-old boy to meet with someone believed to be a minor, with the possible intention of making the boy a part of the sexual tryst. Another predator actually offered Perverted Justice a reference to prove his innocence. The reference was a fourteen-year-old boy he molested in North Dakota before moving to New York. Perverted Justice contacted the police and the predator received convictions in both states. When asked how predators could be so brazen, Von Erck stated, "they know it's wrong, but they do it anyway; they just believe there are more kids than there are police."

And while ongoing national publicity is making Perverted Justice a household brand, Von Erck's unassuming and humble nature keeps the media spotlight in perspective. "Whether or not the media is there, we're doing what we do every day." It's a brand promise that he will keep and one on which our world depends.

Brandstorming Questions

1. What can my company do to make an impact on the local community?

2. Would this be a point of differentiation or simply a component of my corporate responsibility – either way, how can I leverage this to support my brand image?

3. How much, if anything, am I willing to invest to make my community a better place? What ROI will this give me and my brand?

The Calm After the Storm

Now that you've completed your brandstorming exercises, take a deep breath. You probably have countless ideas on various ways you can proceed. Revisit this list when you are ready to make some decisions as to which strategies and tactics you would like to incorporate into your final brand plan. Circle those that you feel will support your brand differentiation. You will revisit these in the last section on the brand plan.

SECTION III:
Planning Your Brand Strategy

CHAPTER 6
Conduct a Communications Audit
(The Big Brown Table Exercise)

"The single biggest problem in communication is the illusion that it has taken place."

—George Bernard Shaw

Clear off the conference room table - you're about to undergo a communications audit. You will want to do this exercise with key members of your organization—sales and marketing managers, senior management team—and even consider doing this with clients and prospects, although those should be conducted in separate focus groups. The communications audit is a first step toward understanding how well your company is communicating your brand. This may take some time depending on the size of your company and its materials, but it's a necessary part of ensuring that you are communicating consistently with all stakeholders.

Collect **ALL** communications from your company - memos, brochures, mailers, letterhead, website pages, and advertisements. Lay them out on the conference room table. Ask yourself the following questions:

☐ Do they all look like they came from the same company?

☐ Do they communicate your brand differentiators?

☐ Is there consistency in each piece in regards to visuals elements, colors, and messaging?

☐ Are there any materials created by your sales team (such as proposals) that look different from standardized company materials?

❏ How do your materials look in relation to your competitor's pieces?

❏ Does anything need an update in terms of message, photography or other elements that make the pieces outdated?

❏ Is the look and feel of the materials consistent with your company? (i.e., a company that sells high end sports cars would have expensive stock, exquisite four-color photography and a luxurious tactile brochure.) A casual diner might have a piece done in one-color printing on plain, cost-effective paper.

❏ Is your language style appropriate for your audience? (For example, if you sell a technology product to people who have limited knowledge of technology, do you speak in a language they can understand? Do you use too much industry terminology and not enough conversational messages?)

❏ Does each department send out materials on their own that don't match the overall look of the brand? (i.e., department newsletters, internal piece, email templates.)

The audit should give you a good idea of where your communication is supporting the brand or falling short of it. You should make a decision on how you are going to proceed with those items that do not support the brand – they should be modified or eliminated. All messages that you send to your clients should give a unified message about who you are.

Some companies put together very sophisticated branding standards manuals to cover every element of the brand and how it should be conveyed: specific colors, fonts, card stock, etc. Depending on the size of your company, you can make your branding standards a simple sheet of elements that must be adhered to. Anyone in the company that is in the position of creating materials should have access to this sheet to ensure that your own employees are not diluting your brand.

CHAPTER 7
Seven Branding Blunders and How to Avoid Them

"If I had to live my life again, I'd make the same mistakes, only sooner."

—Tallulah Bankhead

We all make mistakes, but knowing the most common ones can help us to prevent some of the most common branding boo-boos.

1. Confusing the product with the brand.

When Coca-Cola replaced their traditional recipe with "New Coke," tens of thousands of consumers complained so vehemently, that the new product was taken off the shelves some seventy-eight days after its introduction. Despite $4 million in taste testing research which indicated that consumers actually preferred the New Coke flavor to regular coke and to Pepsi, the new flavor failed. Why? Because people didn't drink Coke for the flavor – they drank it for the brand. Coca-Cola is an all American brand. Coca-Cola is what we drank as children at baseball games and roller skating rinks. Norman Rockwell included Santa Claus drinking Coca-Cola in one of his famous prints. The flavor of traditional Coke is what Americans associate with their youth, their country and their traditions. By changing the recipe, a lifetime of memories was dismantled. And consumers protested. They wanted the old recipe that was familiar to them.

People don't buy products –they buy brands. Do people buy a McDonald's burger because it's the best tasting hamburger around? Do they buy Starbucks because it's the most delicious cup of coffee they've ever tasted? Perhaps, but people often buy brands that make a statement about them. People buy McDonald's because it's family-fun, fast food. They buy Starbucks for the social interaction, trendy atmosphere and upwardly mobile professional vibe. If you confuse the product with the brand, you could get burned. If you're only selling a product or service, then you will look like everyone else. Learn why your customers purchase your product. Then sell the brand, not the product.

2. Inconsistency in the brand message.

Some companies change their message frequently. Ad copy, taglines, even colors change. This often happens because the company gets bored with the message. If you want to have brand consistency, know that you will get bored with your message long before your client does. No one is bored with Nike's "Just Do It." The Maytag "lonely repairman" was a brand favorite that represented dependability for years. The company later changed their differentiation from reliability (which was becoming a commodity feature) to innovation. But the point is that a relevant message will stand the test of time. Consumers rely on consistency. When your message changes frequently, people may think you've changed. Don't change your message. Know that consistency brings security and trust in your brand.

Do you think the Ritz-Carlton is tired of its logo? What if they got bored and decided to change the distinguished, classic graphic? If they did this, customers would be taken aback. They would wonder if something else had changed. People know that wherever they are in the world, they can get world class service at a Ritz-Carlton, but if the luxury hotel were to constantly change its image or logo messaging consumers could have a variety of reactions from confused to suspicious to frustrated. Changes in the look might suggest a change in the brand promise. Consumers don't want to be surprised when they make a purchase. Avoid the urge to change your message. After going through the exercises in this book, choose a brand identity that works and stick with it.

The only time the brand should change is if it is clearly not working, or if changes in time, technology or other circumstances render the brand message ineffective or obsolete. And, even under those circumstances, companies should first consider modifications or a streamline of the message. Only if the brand is deemed completely unusable should a brand makeover occur. The processes in this book can be started from the beginning, taking into account those changes which rendered the brand obsolete. With this knowledge a new brand can be created. Refer to the Vistage article (Strategy #20) from our list of thirty-five companies. It will remind you that changing an element of your brand and message is no small task. Consult a professional.

3. Thinking their company isn't really different than their competitors.

Every time I speak on branding, at least one member of the audience will approach me and say, "This branding stuff is great, but my business is different – I really don't have a point of differentiation, I sell real estate, public relations, financial services," or fill in the industry of your choice. I always tell them that we all sell commodities. And, in fact, many of the world's top brands are commodities with either real or perceived differentiators:

- Chiquita bananas
- Contadina tomatoes
- Green Giant vegetables
- Dole pineapples

If these products can differentiate themselves, so can you! If you don't think your product is different, neither will your clients and you will end up in "no brand's land." And remember, perceived differences are just as powerful as actual differences. Sometimes your most obvious differences are unknown to you! During one of my workshops on branding, an attendee, who was a salesperson in Los Angeles, raised his hand and said, "I'm new to this business

– I don't have any points of differentiation." With the help of the class, I probed a bit deeper into his special strengths and talents. It turns out that this young man was fluent in writing and speaking five languages! Working in the culturally diverse city of Los Angeles, this is quite a differentiator; the percentage of people who can speak five languages is small. The only thing he wasn't doing was leveraging this – he didn't think of it as a powerful difference! So many times, we do not see our own strengths because they come naturally to us and we are too close to them. It is often easier for us to identify our weaknesses. Once this attendee became aware that this was a strength, he was able to leverage his company around this. Some tactics could include creating marketing materials in various languages to key groups, putting flags representing the five languages spoken posted on his website or direct mail pieces, and advertising in newspapers written in these languages. This type of advertising is much more cost effective than running ads in the larger publications. He can also join networking groups in which these languages are spoken. Remember, your differentiator is only a differentiator when you leverage the organization around it.

4. Being out of touch with clients' perceptions of the brand.

Your clients are the most valuable reality check your business has. Ask them for their opinions. Ask them why they buy your product – they may have identified a differentiator you're not even aware of. Ask them what they like and dislike about interacting with your company. Whether it's a phone interview, a card sent through the mail or a focus group, there is a wealth of knowledge available to you from the very people who have chosen your product.

Make sure you keep your surveys simple. People don't want to spend a large amount of time on the phone or filling out a survey. Only you can decide which questions to ask, but be sure to ask what customer loyalty expert Fred Reichheld calls "the ultimate question": "How likely are you to recommend our company to others?"

Reichheld matched responses to this question from tens of thousands of consumers with their actual purchasing behavior. He believes that the answer can help you accurately gauge customer loyalty and predict your company's growth. Reichheld gave clients a ten-point scale to answer the questions and categorized their answers as follows:

- **Promoters** –those who answered the question with ratings of 9 or 10
- **Passives** – those who answered 7 or 8
- **Detractors** – those who answered with a 0 to 6

By subtracting the percentage of detractors from the percentage of promoters, you will get your Net Promoter Score (NPS). Those companies known for world-class customer loyalty have scores in the 50-80 percent range. Average companies have an NPS between 5 and 10 percent. You can use the score to gauge your company as a whole or different division, if you have a larger company. You can also use it as a benchmark to compare your company against competitors if you survey those who purchase from your competition.

The system was used by Intuit, the creators of TurboTax, to boost their sales by 27 percent. They found that detractors were unhappy with post-sale tech support. Passives complained about the rebate process. By correcting these elements, they were able to increase 27 percent in per unit sales and increase their NPS by 5 percent. They also benefited by a 23 percent increase in new customers and a 6 percent increase in market share. If you can only ask one question, this is the one. Also make sure to get their narrative response along with their numeric response. In this way, you will be getting both logical and emotional responses – both are reflections of your brand.

5.   Brand dilution via the sales force.

At the risk of making a lot of enemies, I have to say that one of the most frequent destroyers of the brand message is the sales team. The larger and more geographically dispersed your sales team is, the greater your risk of brand dilution.

A study by Booz Allen has shown that 85 percent of brand selection and loyalty take place from the point of sales contact and afterwards; only 15 percent takes place by up front promotions and the quality of the product itself. Unfortunately, much of the materials created by marketing are never seen by the client during that sales meeting – at least not in their original format. Because salespeople spend as much as sixty hours per month changing marketing materials, cutting and pasting from previous presentations, adding their own graphics, creating their own taglines, or changing the message in some way. They end up with a patchwork quilt of messages that are outdated, inaccurate or just not the brand message that the company wants to convey. They are using a self-designed mish-mosh at the most crucial point of the sales process, the point at which 85 percent of brand decisions will be made! If there is one brand element that keeps me up at night, this is it.

It's not an intentional wish to destroy the brand on the part of the sales team. They just want to customize their presentations for their client. But the result is a fragmented brand message that focuses more on the salesperson than the company.

If you have a small sales team or a one-man operation, you're in luck. But as your company grows, put systems in place to ensure consistency in the PowerPoints and materials that the sales team will use. At Sperry Van Ness, we created a program called *Online.Publisher*, a software program which enables the sales team to input information about the client, the specific information on the property for sale, and other information relevant to the client. At the push of a button, the program generates a brand-friendly proposal. The general brand messages are kept intact along with the graphics, layout, and design. The salesperson can change the content without changing the branding. Programs like this will help you keep control of the brand when it's most important—at the point of sales contact.

6. Breaking the brand promise.

While traveling in Bolivia in 2000, I learned the power of keeping the brand promise. I was hungry and it was time for lunch. Locals told me to carefully choose where I ate—the quality of the meat and the cleanliness of preparation could vary greatly. All of a sudden, something as simple as eating lunch became a risky proposition. And then, I saw them—the Golden Arches of McDonald's—and I knew everything was going to be okay. I knew that by going to McDonald's, I could rely on their brand promise: a hot, tasty, and predictable meal that would taste the same in Bolivia as it did in the U.S. I ordered my Big Mac and diet Coke – and, yes, it tasted exactly as predicted. There was even an internet kiosk in the middle of the restaurant that enabled me to check my email. Many people in the area do not have their own computers and rely on those businesses that provide them. And McDonald's delivered.

Keeping your brand promise gives your consumers assurance of a consistent and predictable experience with your product. The predictability is what will enable them to make a choice not only to purchase your product, but in many cases to pay more for the brand experience than they would for your non-branded competitors.

One sure way to break the brand promise is to fail to empower employees to carry the brand message through. Some hotels give each employee a budget of up to $100 per client to resolve complaints on the spot. So, if a guest snags her panty hose on a table, the employee is empowered to fix the problem without having to get permission from management. Knowing that they can make decisions to resolve customer complaints without repercussions enables the employee to ensure the brand message is carried through. Make sure that you have systems in place to ensure that you can keep your promises. Your brand depends on it.

7. Not providing a unique experience.

Don't confuse an ordinary product with ordinary experiences. Anything can be made memorable. I recently went to a hair salon for a cut. While paying for my bill, I decided to purchase a bottle of shampoo. The girl at the desk wrapped the bottle in colorful tissue paper, sealed the paper with a silver foil seal, and then put it in a beautiful paper bag with handles and a curled ribbon on it. It was just a bottle of shampoo, but it looked like a present! It was such a small gesture that made me feel special. Creating a remarkable experience is often in the details. Other companies I have observed who create remarkable experiences:

a. An orthodontist who gives patients who have had their braces removed a mug of all the candy they can't eat while wearing braces – chewy, sticky and hard candies like Sugar Babies, caramels, licorice, jaw breakers, and candy bars. After giving the mug, he takes a photo of himself with the patient and puts it on his wall.

b. An auto dealership that takes a picture of the client standing next to their new car. About one week after the purchase, a large calendar bearing the photo is sent to the client. The photo remains while each month of the calendar is used. It's an attractive piece that will not likely get tossed and will serve as a reminder of the purchase experience.

c. A real estate agent who sends his clients stationery bearing an artistic rendering of their home.

d. A chiropractor that plays your favorite music while giving you a massage and uses heated pads to position your arms and feet so there are no uncomfortable pressure points as you receive the treatment.

e. An auto service center that calls the client a few days after the service to ask five short questions about the experience and see if there is anything else they can provide for the client.

CHAPTER 8
ACTING on Brand Challenges

*"Challenges are gifts that force us to search for a new center of gravity.
Don't fight them. Just find a different way to stand."*
—Oprah Winfrey

You will have some challenges as you pursue a powerful brand. Remember them through the acronym, ACTING:

A	ADD of consumers
C	Cynicism
T	Tyranny of Choice
I	Imitators
N	New Technology
G	Growth

A   ADD of Consumers

Don't blame your clients and prospects for having **ADD** (Attention Deficit Disorder). It's not their fault. They're bombarded with 3000 or more messages each day from radio, television, billboards, and the internet. Your messages must be powerful and consistent. We're numb to most of these messages and often they don't stand out without an immense amount of repetition. A major retailer ran a new ad campaign during the *2006 Academy*

Awards show. Their ad ran sixteen times during the program. And that was only one event. This can give you a sense of how important repetition is, and how expensive. Advertising is powerful, but unless you can have a dominant position, consider other methods that may be able to accomplish what you need.

I often have frustrated business owners telling me, "I ran an ad and didn't get any calls." These are not rookie business owners, these are people who make six figure incomes. What they don't understand—and what I tell them repeatedly—is that advertising is like weightlifting. You would never walk into a gym and lift one weight, one time and expect to get results. Reach (the percentage of your target audience that saw the ad) and frequency (the number of times they saw the ad) are two things that impact your advertising, with, in my opinion, frequency being the more important of the two. Think of reach as the number of pounds of the freeweight you are lifting, and frequency as the number of repetitions with the weight. This will give you an idea of how advertising works. Weightlifting must provide a significant amount of weight and frequency in order to get a result. I tell people, if you can't create a campaign with repetition, don't waste your money. If you do not have the money to spend on advertising get through to your prospects using special events by working with your local media, email campaigns or a direct mail program.

C   Cynicism

Consumers have also become cynical of advertising and sales and the Internet has made them more savvy consumers than ever before. Consumers have heard about features and benefits. They're used to having accessibility to a multitude of products available to them and they know that if your product doesn't cut it, they can find another one that will. Cynicism of the consumer means you may not have a second chance to impress a client with your product. Now, more than ever, it is important to get it right the first time.

T   Tyranny of Choice

In *Differentiate or Die,* Jack Trout refers to the "tyranny of choice" of today's consumer. Even though an average family has most of its needs met by 150 SKU's (standard stocking units) in a supermarket, the average super-market has 40,000 SKU's. We can choose from 340 breakfast cereals, eighty-seven soft drink brands and fifty bottled water brands. Those that are chosen have learned to cut through the clutter and be noticed. You will constantly be faced with the challenge of how to do just that.

I   Imitators

The good news is you've launched a great brand. The bad news is you will be imitated. Even if you are the first mover in your category, it doesn't ensure that you will prevail. Success draws competition. And while it may be the sincerest form of flattery, competition can be a threat if your competitors do a better job of selling themselves than you do. Often, competitors will imitate your product and perhaps add a feature or two. Another competitor comes along and does the same thing. By the time the third version of a product comes along, only 15 percent of first movers are still in the number one position. This is why the VRIO model is so important—it includes consideration of the imitation factor.

N   New Technology

Any advancement in technology can make your product obsolete. And you don't have to be in the technology business for this to occur. When the Internet came into being and customers began shopping online, brick and mortar retailers suddenly had to incorporate an online component to keep shoppers. Online video rentals changed the way people shopped for DVDs. Know that whatever your product is, it will be important to gauge the impact of new technology on how your clients view it, access it or use it.

G   Growth

We all strive for growth, but sometimes growth can happen quickly and impair our ability to provide the same services that brought customers to us in the first place. Have a plan for growth. Know how you will be able to accommodate new clients, build infrastructure, leverage vendor relationships, and provide the same level of quality and customer service that prompted your growth.

CHAPTER 9
Putting It All Together: The Plan

"Plans are only good intentions unless they immediately
degenerate into hard work."
—Peter Drucker

You're now ready to crate a brand plan. You will be able to complete most of this plan by referring to the exercises you have already completed in the book. The plan is decidedly simple; because complicated business plans often end up looking really impressive as they collect dust on your bookshelf. I used to work for a Fortune 500 company and every year for six years, I had to create a very specific type of marketing plan. It was the size of a New York City phone book. While the process of creating the plan was educational, the plan itself was rarely referenced. That's because we had excellent systems and metrics that we used on a daily or even hourly basis to help us make decisions. Do your research; it will help you understand where you need to go. But create a plan that is brief enough that you can reference daily, and modify as needed. By going through the process of planning, you will create clarity of purpose for your managers and employees to motivate them to move forward.

The Brand Plan

Brand Plan for _____

(company name)

Date_____

What business are we in?

Who are our clients?

Who are our competitors?

What do we sell?

What other valuable services does our company offer that will not be promoted as our primary brand differentiator but are still valuable? (Include anything valuable from the **VRIO** exercise.) Since these are not points of differentiation, they are points of parity; we will still communicate them to clients, but not as part of the primary message.

Elements of our Brand

(Add these from the original exercise, or modify.)

Visual

Emotional

Rational

Cultural

Our proprietary products, trademarks, patents, registrations:

The following are items which have not been trademarked but will be shortly:

VRIO Analysis

Our company's single greatest differentiator as evidenced by our VRIO analysis, and the one that we will choose to promote is:

This differentiator will be reviewed regularly to ensure that it still meets VRIO criteria. This differentiator supports my company's vision statement, culture and values, and overall strategy.

My differentiator is

Valuable because

Rare because

Costly or difficult to imitate because

Our primary strategy to promote our differentiation is (you can use any of the strategies from the Brandstorming session or create your own)

Tactics we will incorporate from the brandstorming session include

Manufacturing (if applicable) is leveraged around the brand by (Check all that apply and add your own. Anything checked should have an explanation of how you will organize this element around the brand).

☐ raw materials _____

☐ capacity _____

☐ location _____

☐ procurement _____

☐ production _____

☐ assembly _____

☐ other _____

Operations are organized around the brand in the following ways: (explain each that is checked)

☐ The president or CEO serves as a brand champion, referencing the brand, in all communications and ensuring that brand message is carried out throughout the organization.

☐ All managers make the brand message a part of their training and department execution.

☐ Specific practices are designed to reinforce the brand message.

Managers should...

☐ Ensure their respective departments can articulate the point of differentiation.

☐ Work with their employees to carry out the differentiator within their respective jobs.

☐ Make business decisions on whether or not they support or negate the brand.

☐ Reinforce the brand messaging in their staff meetings and interactions by empowering employees to take care of customer needs on the spot and will support them for doing so.

☐ Other _____

Marketing, Public Relations & Communications are leveraged to support the differentiator by: (explain each item that is checked)

☐ Completing a communications audit.

☐ Ensuring consistency in all communications—print, electronic, website, media, advertising—in terms of tone, content, messaging, and graphics.

☐ Working with the media to place stories that communicate our differentiators.

☐ Conducting special events, trade shows, and other activities that communicate the brand promise.

☐ Creating and enforcing a brand standards manual to be used company wide.

☐ Ensuring all materials communicate the point of differentiation.

☐ Ensuring the visual and tactile quality of the marketing materials convey a tone and quality equal to or greater than the quality of my services.

☐ Ensuring graphics and messaging are consistent over time unless there is a specific reason for changing.

Sales is leveraged to support the differentiator by: (explain each item that is checked)

☐ A standard script, story or sales approach that my sales team uses to communicate the differentiators of my company.

☐ The sales pitch is persuasive and triggers key emotions that prompt action.

☐ System are in place to ensure that my sales team does not create or customize their materials in a way that alters the brand.

☐ Other: _____

The Act of **Completing the transaction** is leveraged around the differentiator by: (explain each item that is checked)

☐ Creating an experience above and beyond the transaction that is remarkable or memorable.

☐ Delivering products and services consistently regardless of whether they are accessed on the web or in person.

☐ Ensuring client's interaction with my product, services and employees is positive, unique and memorable because:

☐ Ensuring that my product or service is easy to use, find or access.

☐ Other: _____

Customer Service is leveraged to support the differentiator by: (explain each item that is checked)

☐ Customer complaints are dealt with in an effective manner.

☐ Customer complaints are shared in a system that will minimize their occurrence in the future.

☐ Customer service is knowledgeable of the brand.

☐ Other systems I will put in place to ensure customer service is leveraged around the brand: _____

Human Resources is leveraged to support the differentiator by:

☐ Employees receive training in the brand and differentiator

☐ Employees can state the company's point of differentiation

☐ Potential employees are aware of the brand by:

☐ Brand differentiation is included in classified ads, at *www.monster.com*, descriptions or any materials handed out at job fairs.

Employees are rewarded for championing the brand by:
  ☐ inclusion in annual reviews
  ☐ rewards- gifts or bonuses
  ☐ recognition

Technology is leveraged to support the differentiator by

☐ Keeping the company up to date with technology, **CRM** systems and other customer needs. Explain.

☐ If I have a technology department, it supports other departments in executing the brand promise.

☐ Assists marketing with website functionality, search engine optimization and web metrics.

☐ Other: _____

Customer Service is leveraged to support the differentiator by:

☐ Surveying customers regularly.

☐ Using information learned to improve the brand experience.

☐ Speaking on the phone in a way that communicates friendliness, accessibility, and knowledge.

☐ Resolving customer service issues promptly and efficiently to the client's satisfaction by:

☐ Percentage of my customer satisfaction ratings that are excellent, well above average or superior _____.

☐ My clients regularly refer others to my company as evidenced by:

☐ My clients use my services consistently and do not flip back and forth between me and my competitors. I know this because:

Pricing is leveraged to support the differentiator by:

☐ I am not the low price leader, my differentiator justifies the higher price? Explain.

☐ I am the low price leader, I realize that this is not a differentiation strategy; it is a low-cost strategy. As such, I realize I must have the volume, vendor relationships or economies of scale that can sustain my company. (Note: low price is not a brand strategy; it is a low price strategy. To prevail, you must be able to continue being the low price leader, or change to a differentiation strategy.)

In a Word

My brand can be defined in a word. The word is _____

If I cannot define my brand in one word, what brief phrase can define my brand?

_____

In what creative way can I describe the word or phrase I own in a catchy, memorable tagline? Write your tagline here. (It is suggested that you decide this with a consultant, your management team, key employees and clients to ensure that it is easily understood and resonates with the consumer.)

My tagline is _____

The Rule of Three's

The three things I have to do in the next year, quarter, month, week that will have the most dramatic impact on my brand are:

Next Year
1.
2.
3.

Next Quarter
1.
2.
3.

Next Month
1.
2.
3.

Next Week
1.
2.
3.

The Rule of Three's Section will be updated regularly to ensure that I am always focusing on the three most important issues that will positively impact my brand. By starting with what needs to happen next year, you can break down your tasks accordingly to ensure that your short term actions will achieve your long term goals. It will often take more than three things to achieve a goal. Create and entire list of things and sort them in the sequence in which they need to be done. When the first three are done, replace them with the next three, and so on.

Conclusion

"Whenever I hear, 'It can't be done,' I know I'm close to success."
—Michael Flatley, Lord of the Dance

You've done it – you've conducted a thorough assessment of your brand. You've learned how to identify a differentiator and execute it through specific tactics. You've learned the right questions to ask and answer to ensure that you are focused on the right things. You've created a brand plan to optimize your success. And now that you've seen the process, doesn't it seem less intimidating and more achievable?

I encourage you to take your brand test six months after implementing your program and again in one year. I know that if you put your plan into practice, you will dramatically increase your Brand Quotient and your ability to have a sustainable competitive advantage in your market.

Tell Me How You're Doing

Please let me know how you're doing. I would love to hear your successes and your challenges. Send stories of your successes and challenges in executing the brand to:

info@sandrasellani.com

You just might be asked to be a part of my next book.

Thank you!

Sandra Sellani

To create your **BQ** grid online, go to *www.mybrandquotient.com*

For general information, visit *www.sandrasellani.com*

References

Books

- Burlingame, Bo. 2005. *Small Giants*. Penguin Group.
- Godin, Seth. 2005. *All Marketers are Liars*. Penguin Publishing.
- Klymshyn, John. 2003. *Move the Sale Forward*. Silver Lake Publishing.
- Lakhani, David. 2005. *Persuasion: The Art of Getting What You Want*. Wiley.
- Levitt, Steven, and Dubner, Stephen. 2005. *Freakonomics*. William Morrow.
- Levitt, S. & Syverson, C. 2005. *Market Distortions when Agents are Better Informed: The Value of Information in Real Estate Transactions*. University of Chicago.
- Marion Kaufman Foundation. 2006. *The Entrepreneur Next Door*.
- Morris, Betsey. 2006. *The New Rules*. Fortune.
- Mack, Ben. 2007. *Think Two Products Ahead: Secrets the Big Advertising Agencies Don't Want You to Know and How to Use Them for Bigger Profits*, Wiley, *www.Wiley.com*.
- Reichheld, Fred. 2006. *The Ultimate Question*. Harvard Business School Press.
- Toffler, Alvin. 1970. *Future Shock*. New York: Bantam Books.
- Trout, Jack, 2000. *Differentiate or Die: Survival in Our Era of Killer Competition*. Wiley.

Booklets

- Mack, Ben. *How to Create a Legend Platform and Turn Every First Sale into Residual Steams of Income*, p. 1.

Brochures

- EGBAR Foundation. 2006. Environmental Fellowship brochure. Simple Green.
- Lazy Bear Ranch Brochure. 2006. Lazy Bear Ranch.

Classes

- Sherman, Scott. Strategy Class, Pepperdine University, May 2003.

Interviews

Alvarez, Guy. May 22, 2006. Interview by Sandra Sellani.

Black, Charley. May 24, 2006. Interview by Sandra Sellani.

Bell, Bob. July 13, 2006. Interview by Sandra Sellani.

Blohm, Peder. July 11, 2006. Interview by Sandra Sellani.

Blohm, Peder and Pais, Andy. July 13, 2006. Interview by Sandra Sellani.

Casser, Conrad and Mitchell, Rory. June 19, 2006. Interview by Sandra Sellani.

Ceccoli, Rich. April 19, 2006. Interview by Sandra Sellani.

DiPietro, Laura. June 28, 2006. Interview by Sandra Sellani.

Eng, Chris and Kim, Doug. May 25, 2006. Interview by Sandra Sellani.

Erskine, Sue. May 17, 2006. Interview by Sandra Sellani.

Fabrizio, Bruce. July 11, 2006. Interview by Sandra Sellani.

Gadbois, Frances and Steele, Jude. June 28, 2006. Interview by Sandra Sellani.

Garfinkel, David and Mack, Ben. July 12, 2006. Interview by Sandra Sellani.

Granito, Diane. June 28, 2006. Interview by Sandra Sellani.

Greer, Neil. June 20, 2006. Interview by Sandra Sellani.

Hargraves, Simon. August 9, 2006. Interview by Sandra Sellani.

Jakeway, Phil. May 22, 2006. Interview by Sandra Sellani.

Katler, Todd. July 7, 2006. Interview by Sandra Sellani.

Klymshyn, John. April 18, 2006. Interview by Sandra Sellani.

Knapp, Geoff. June 22, 2006. Interview by Sandra, Sellani.

Knorp, Scott. June 22, 2006. Interview by Sandra Sellani.

Lakhani, Dave. July 6, 2006. Interview Sandra Sellani.

Lam, Wing. June 30, 2006. Interview by Sandra Sellani.

Machat, Michael. June 19, 2006. Interview by Sandra Sellani.

Morales, Daniel. July 6, 2006. Interview by Sandra Sellani.

Neufeld, Michael. April 15, 2006. Interview by Sandra Sellani.

Pick, Doug. June 27, 2006. Interview by Sandra Sellani.

Qubein, Nido. June 28, 2006. Interview by Sandra Sellani.

Rosas, Cesar. June 27, 2006. Interview by Sandra Sellani.

Shanahan, Doreen. June 20, 2006. Interview by Sandra Sellani.

Stahl, Jack. May 29, 2006. Interview by Sandra Sellani.

Swasey, Steve. June 22, 2006. Interview by Sandra Sellani.

Von Erck, Xavier. June 2, 2006. Interview by Sandra Sellani.

Wrightman, Tim. June 14, 2006. Interview by Sandra.

Young, Tim. July 14, 2006. Interview by Sandra Sellani.

Magazine Articles

- Coster, Helen. June 19, 2006. Not So Fine Wine. *Forbes Magazine*: 86 – 88.
- Gunther, Marc. August 7, 2006. The Green Machine. *Fortune Magazine*: 42-57.
- Kotkin, Joel. March 2004. Top 25 Cities for Doing Business In America. *Inc.* Magazine: 93.

  July/August 2005. Top 100 Small Businesses. *Fortune Small Business Magazine*.
- Seiler, Marianne. November/December 2005. High Performance: To become a market leader, you must master five Critical factors. *Marketing Management*: 19-23.
- Overman, Stephenie. April – June 2006. Show Off Your Brand. *Staffing Management Magazine*: 25 – 27.
- Wasserman, Todd. June 19, 2006. Superbrands '06. Brandweek, Vol. XLVII, No.25: 67-70.
- Zibart, Rosemary. October 15, 2006. Their Faces Spoke to the Heart. *Parade.com. http://www.parade.com/articles/editions/2005/edition 01-02-2005/featured 0*

Marketing Presentations

- Marketing Presentation, September 2005, The Sperry Van Ness Difference.

Newsletters

- Golembeski, Thomas, Editor in Chief, *The Marketing Report*, Progressive Business Publications, Malvern, PA. March 6, 2006.

Online Publications

- Lavelle, L, Gloeckler, G., Gerdes, L. *The Best Executive MBA's*, October 24, 2006. *www.businessweekonline.com.*
- MacMillan, Douglas. Minting Women Millionaires. *Business Week Online* July 3, 2006: 1. *http://www.businessweek.com/smallbiz/content/may2006.*
- Pret's Hunger for Quality Starts with Staff Recruitment. *South China Morning Post*, Saturday 31st May, 2003. *www.classifiedpost.com.*
- The Brookings Institution, Metropolitan Policy Program, Living Cities, *Philadelphia in Focus: A Profile from Census 2000*, November 2003. *www.brookings.edu.*

Press Releases
- Velázquez Press. "Geno's Steaks in Philadelphia gets a Spanish and English Dictionary." Press Release, June 13, 2006, *www.velazquezpress.com.*

Radio Shows

- Handle, Bill, KFI-640 Radio Show. Thursday, June 17, 2004. *Success from Scratch Series.*
- Liasson, Mara. June 22, 2006. *Immigration Debate Divides Republican Congress.* National Public Radio. *www.npr.org/templates/story/story.php?storyId=5503155*

Reports

- Target Corporation. June 16, 2006. *Corporate Responsibility Report.*

TV News

- Hunter, Greg & McCabe, Kim. June 16, 2006 *Lawsuit asks: is your sunscreen doing its job?* CNN.
- Wells, Jane. June 30, 2006, *Junk Worth Stealing*. CNBC Business News. Los Angeles.

Websites

- About Nido Qubein. 2006. Nido Qubein's official Website. *http://www.nido-qubein.com/aboutnidoqubein.cfm*
- About Our Company. Pret a Manger. *http://www.pret.com/about/*
- About Sperry Van Ness. Sperry Van Ness. *http://www.svn.com/Default.aspx?pgid=8*
- About Us. Laptop Design USA. *http://laptopdesignusa.com/content/view/12/26/*
- A Laptop with the Brand of You. 9/20/2005, Made for One.com, *http://www.madeforone.com/News/20050926-Laptop-Design.html*
- America's Best Colleges 2007. U.S. News and World Report. *http://www.usnews.com/usnews/edu/college/rankings/brief/t1natudoc_brief.php*
- Archives. Online Conversation Transcripts Between WB Sooner and Fancy Dancer. *http://www.perverted-justice.com/?archive=WBSooner*
- Articles: Moving Conversations Forward. 2003. The Business Generator, *http://www.klymshyn.com/index.php*
- Badenhausen, Kurt and Kump, Lesley. Special Report: Best Business Schools, August 18, 2005. Forbes. *http://www.forbes.com/careers/2005/08-/16/best-business-schools-list-cz_05mba_land.html*
- BDI Wingspan Services. Business Development Institute. *http://www.bdionline.com/services/wingspan.asp*
- blink-182, 2006. AbsolutePunk . *http://www.absolutepunk.net/artists/showlink.php?do=showdetails&l=1754*
- Bold Approach Services. Bold Approach, *http://www.boldapproach.com/services.html*
- Bramhall, Joe. Pret a Manger (Europe) LTD. Hoovers.com,

http://www.hoovers.com/pret-a-manger/--ID__103213--/free-co-factsheet.xhtml

- Browse: At a Glance:, Felicity Season 1. Netflix .
  http://www.netflix.com/MovieDisplay?movieid=60030530&trkid=189530&strki-d=333583330_6_0

- California Pinot Noir. October 3, 2005. Wine Institute.
  http://www.wineinstitute.org/industry/consumer/pinot_noir.php

- Character Story Development Projects, Maytag Corporation. The Maytag Repairman, Character, LLC. *http://www.characterweb.com/maytag.html*

- Church of Tom Jones: Spiritual Awakenings. Church of Tom Jones.
  http://www.churchoftomjones.com/churchoftomjones.asp

- Community Bank Ventures, LLC Appoints Cesar Rosas to Executive Vice President, Director of Emerging Bank Markets. June 2, 2006. Community Bank Ventures. *http://www.communitybankventures.com/news.html*

- Company Information. CAM Commerce Solutions. *http://www.camcommerce.com/company/*

- Company. MBT: The History, Swiss Masai US, LLC. *http://www.swissmasaius.com/History.aspx*

- Company Overview. Vistage. *http://www.vistage.com/about-us.html*

- eBay, Inc. Hoovers. *http://www.hoovers.com/ebay/--ID__56307--/free-co-factsheet.xhtml*

- Exxon Valdez. Updated March 8, 2006. U.S. Environmental Protection Agency. *http://www.epa.gov/oilspill/exxon.htm*

- Faith Based Finance: About Faith and Community @ Work. Nubank.
  http://www.nubank.com/faithbased/faithcommunity.html

- FAQ:How VoIP, Internet Voice Works. Federal Communications Commission. *www.fcc.gov/voip/*

- Features: Dental Exec. 2006. Dental-Exec. *http://www.dentalexec.com/dental-exec/features.html*

- Features: Oral Surgery-Exec. 2006. Oral Surgery-Exec.
  http://www.oralsurgeryexec.com/oralsurgery-exec/v11/features.html

- Graziadio School of Business and Management. E2B: Connecting Education to Business. Pepperdine University. *http://bschool.pepperdine.edu/programs/e2b/*

- Handel, Bill. News, Media and Events: Success From Scratch. Radio Show, KFI-AM, June 17, 2004. Simple Green.

http://consumer.simplegreen.com/cons_news_med_kfi_am_640_2.php

- Home Page, Entrepreneur's Organization, *http://www.eonetwork.org/*

- Home Page. Official Website for Ben Mack's Book, *Think Two Products Ahead, www.thinktwoproductsahead.com*

- Home Page. Persuasion: The Art of Getting What You Want. Lakhani, Dave. 2006. *http://www.howtopersuade.com/home.html*

- Immigrant Banking and Emerging Markets. Nubank. *http://www.nubank.com/immigrants/index.html*

- Islamic Banking. Nubank. *http://www.nubank.com/islamic/index.html*

- Kodak Dental Systems: Simplify Your Practice. Kodak. *http://www.kodak.com/global/en/health/dental/index.jhtml?pq-path=2146*

- Kodak Health Group. 2006. Hoovers. *http://www.hoovers.com/kodak-health-group/--ID__138056--/free-co-factsheet.xhtml*

- Letter from Tim Wrightman. Lazy Bear Ranch. *http://www.lazybearranch.com/index.php*

- Links. Sector 9. *http://www.sector9.com/2006/*

- Member Demographics. Vistage. *http://www.vistage.com/about-us/member-demographics.html*

- Message from the Office of the President. High Point University, 2006. Nido R. Qubein. A *http://www.highpoint.edu/administration/president*

- Native American Bankers; There has never been a better time to pursue tribal ownership. Native American Bankers. *http://www.nativeamericanbankers.com/*

- Otto Von Bismark Quotes. BrainyQuote. *http://www.brainyquote.com/quotes/quotes/o/ottovonbis134222.html*

- Person: Travis Barker, 2006. TV.com. *http://www.tv.com/search.php?qs=Travis+Barker&type=11&stype=all&tag=search%3Bbutton*

- Peter Drucker Quotes. Thinkexist.com. *http://en.thinkexist.com/quotes/peter_drucker/2.html*

- Product Information. Progressive Universal Life Church. *http://www.pulc.com/products.php*

- Riesterer, Tim. "Exploring the Territory Known as No Brand's Land", August 5, 2003, MarketingProfs.com, *http://www.marketingprofs.com/3/riesterer1.asp*

- Robbins, Perry Dr. "Beauty Q&A: Sun Protection Pills." Cosmopolitan. *http://magazines.ivillage.com/cosmopolitan/style/confess/qas/0,,426395_697025*

,00.html

- Running Shoe Blog. "US Sales of Athletic Footwear Rose 2.8 percent", posted by Kevin Tiller, Monday, February 26, 2006. Runners Wordpress.com. *http://runners.wordpress.com/?s=US+Sales+of+Athletic+Footwear*

- Sector 9 Longboards- The Complete Long Skate Board. 2006. Soul Boards. *http://www.soulboards.com/sector9longboardskateboard.htm*

- See Pastor Jack on VH1's Totallly Obsessed! Church of Tom Jones. *http://www.churchoftomjones.com/*

- Skin Cancer Facts. October 18, 2006, Skin Cancer Foundation, *http://www.skin-cancer.org/skincancer-facts.php.*

- Skin Cancer Fact Sheet. American Academy of Dermatology. *http://www.aad.org/aad/Newsroom/skincancerfact.htm*

- Skin Cancer Resource Center. September 27, 2006. Medscape Today *http://www.medscape.com/resource/skincancer*

- Spanish in the United States. August 8, 2006. Wikipedia.com. *http://en.wikipedia.org/wiki/Spanish_in_the_United_States*

- Sunpill Information. Pure Pharmaceuticals, LLC. *http://www.sunpill.com/sunpill-information.cfm*

- The U.S. Luxury Market Continues to Boom. Unity Marketing. May 2006. Research and Markets. p. 250. *http://www.researchandmarkets.com/reportinfo.asp?cat_id=0&report_id=338962&q=US%20Luxury%20Market&p=1*

- Tim Wrightman's official Website. About Tim. *www.timwrightman.com*

- Tools. Freerealtime.com. h*ttp://quotes.freerealtime.com/dl/frt/T?toparea=Tools*

- Velázquez Press. *http://www.velazquezpress.com/*

- Wahoo's Story, 2006. Wahoo's Fish Taco. *www.wahoos.com*

- Waters, Shari. Retailing: Top Four Sources of Shrinkage. About.com. *http://retail.about.com/od/lossprevention/tp/shrink_sources.htm?terms=Retailing+Shrinkage*

- Work: DSN: Underlying Story. 2006. Dovecote. *www.dovecoteny.com*

Index

THIS BOOK DOESN'T STOP AT THE LAST PAGE!

We want to hear from you!

Join our email list to continue your experience.

WBusiness Books is not just a business book publisher, it's a community for business readers who learn and share their experiences.
Sign up for our mailing list at
www.Wbusinessbooks.com and join the WBusiness Community.